Contents

Rosenwald Hall tower

The University of Chicago campus, 1905

Preface

On a Saturday afternoon, the first day of October of 1892, William Rainey Harper assembled the faculty of the University of Chicago for its first meeting. They met in what was then the "chapel," a large room in Cobb Hall, still under construction and the only classroom and office building under roof. Its windows overlooked the swamp that was to be developed into our campus.

The importance of the occasion appeared overwhelming to those present who sensed that this newly created university would change American higher education as none other has. Even Charles R. Henderson, the University Recorder, failed to take minutes. But Marion Talbot, a member of the faculty and Dean of Women in the Colleges, kept some notes. Harper, she said, opened the meeting with a prayer and then in his remarks to his colleagues stated that the question before the faculty was how to become one in spirit, if not necessarily one in opinion.

One in spirit, if not in opinion, has been a hallmark of our University for 100 years, a hallmark of a faculty and student body deeply committed to the enterprise, but disagreeing on all kinds of issues on any street corner in Hyde Park, at the tables in the Quad-rangle Club, or in the various commons, libraries, classrooms and laboratories. In 100 years, Chicago has made for itself a culture that is cohesive, rigorous, and tough. No one leaves here, really. Away from it physically, memory of it remains. Its influence in this and many other ways is felt throughout the academic world.

The expository history which follows and which captures those characteristics had its own beginnings in an exhibition arranged by the late Robert Rosenthal, Curator of Special Collections of the University Library, in the autumn of 1973. The exhibition was not to be a history, he said, but "an arrangement of documentation and iconographic resources for the history of an institution." It had Bob Rosenthal's personal, engaging touch and his broad sense of the

University, of its importance and what is important to say about it. The text for the original exhibition catalogue was written by Albert M. Tannler.

We decided to recast the catalogue to recreate it as a brief account of the University's history and to bring it up to date. No one could perform such a task better than Robert E. Streeter, the Edward L. Ryerson Distinguished Service Professor Emeritus in the Department of English Language and Literature and the College and former Dean of the Division of the Humanities. Robert Streeter did not want it called a "history." For him this book reflects some observations about the University. It also demonstrates his elegance of expression and his love for and understanding of the University. He is one in spirit with Bob Rosenthal and with so many others who have devoted themselves to the University and its community.

I welcome you to this introduction to Chicago, knowing I will receive many opinions about it. The spirit of Chicago remains true to what a university should be, as it always has and always will.

Hanna Holborn Gray
Autumn 1991

On opposite page: Botany Pond with Hull Gate in background

The Old University of Chicago
(Douglas Hall)

The Founding of the University

According to popular legend, the University of Chicago sprang into the world fully formed when it opened its doors in 1892, the product of John D. Rockefeller's oil millions, Marshall Field's land, and the vision of a young Biblical scholar from Yale, William Rainey Harper. In actuality, the founding of the University culminated a complex and lengthy negotiation involving a number of persons, Rockefeller and Harper prominent among them, who were united in the dream of establishing a great center of higher learning in the Midwest.

For two and a half centuries American religious bodies had established colleges to ensure an educated clergy and responsive laymen. Some of these denominational colleges evolved into universities. It was not surprising that Chicago Baptists shared this religious concern for the support of higher education. Even before the Civil War, in 1856, they had joined Stephen A. Douglas in establishing what came to be known as the Old University of Chicago on land donated by Douglas on the South Side. Although the institution survived for three decades, it failed to secure an adequate endowment. Unable to meet its obligations to its principal creditor, the old University held its last convocation on June 16, 1886.

The struggle to save the old University, however, had attracted the attention of an influential Baptist layman, John D. Rockefeller, and the hope of reviving the institution under more favorable auspices was maintained through the efforts of several far-sighted Baptist educators. The correspondence between Rockefeller and these educators documents a remarkable series of discussions and meetings, between 1887 and 1890, during which the plans to reestablish the University took firm shape. Four of the prime movers—Thomas W. Goodspeed, William Rainey Harper, Frederick T. Gates, and Henry L. Morehouse—were in frequent communication and, though not of one mind, evolved a plan to present to Rockefeller, the one man they believed capable of making the new University a reality.

Stephen A. Douglas

Historically decentralized because of their commitment to the autonomy of individual congregations, the Baptists had nonetheless created several denominational agencies to advance their interests. Morehouse was executive officer of one of these, the American Home Mission Society, to which was entrusted the supervision of educational institutions. In June 1887, Morehouse persuaded the Mission Society to recommend the establishment of a new denominational agency to direct Baptist resources to new and existing schools and colleges. In 1888, the American Baptist Education Society was founded under the leadership of Gates, a clergyman from Minneapolis who had been successful in educational fundraising. As Gates began a thorough examination of the denomination's educational needs, his attention was attracted to the Middle West, the area in which the number of Baptist congregations was increasing most markedly. Coming to Chicago to study the situation at first hand, Gates met with George W. Northrup and Goodspeed, president and trustee respectively of the Baptist Union Theological Seminary, and learned of a plan to reestablish the old university near the seminary campus in suburban Morgan Park.

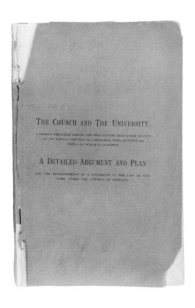

Gates was soon convinced that Chicago—by virtue of setting, population growth, and resources—was the preferred location. Yet he realized that the failure of the earlier university had bred caution among members of the Baptist community who possessed the financial resources needed for the new enterprise. A major gift from Rockefeller would no doubt reassure the local community, but Rockefeller's "last and final word," Gates wrote to Morehouse on July 14, 1888, "is that he will not take the initiative, and will not make any propositions." Clearly, Rockefeller wanted to be sure that Chicago Baptists were in earnest.

The first sign that Rockefeller looked with favor on a new university in Chicago came in a letter of October 13, 1888, to Goodspeed from Professor William Rainey Harper of Yale University. Rockefeller had unexpectedly appeared at Vassar (where Harper taught a weekly course), and the philanthropist and the scholar discussed the proposed university at Chicago for thirteen hours:

He stands ready after the holidays to do something for Chicago. It will have to be managed, however, very carefully; but the chief point of my letter is this: In our discussion of the general question he showed great interest in the Educational Society (I mean the new one) and above all talked for hours in reference to the scheme of establishing the great university at Chicago instead of in New York. This surprised me very much. As soon as I began to see how the matter struck him I pushed it and I lost no opportunity of emphasizing this point. The long and

George W. Northrup

short of it is I feel confident that his mind has turned, and that it is a possible thing to have the money which he proposed to spend in New York diverted to Chicago.

The "great university" scheme to which Harper referred was an idea advanced by the Reverend Dr. Augustus A. Strong, president of the Rochester Theological Seminary and an in-law of Rockefeller. Strong believed that the greatest educational need of the Baptists was a well-endowed university in New York City devoted exclusively to graduate work. He vigorously urged this project on Rockefeller. Harper apparently assumed that Rockefeller was committed to funding an institution of such scope; indeed, Rockefeller may have introduced the topic in positive terms in order to elicit Harper's opinion. What surprised Harper was Rockefeller's interest in Chicago's educational needs and his possible intention of meeting them.

Meanwhile, the sentiment of the American Baptist Education Society was beginning to crystallize in favor of a university in Chicago. Speaking at a Baptist ministers' conference in Chicago on October 15, 1888, Gates read a paper titled "The Need of a Baptist University of Chicago, as Illustrated by a Study of Baptist Collegiate Education in the West." He reported the phenomenal growth of the Baptist denomination in the Middle West, noted the small number of Baptist colleges "fixed in small obscure towns, surrounded by a most worthy but wholly impecunious population," and referred to the frequent loss of college-age young people to the schools of other denominations. After surveying possible remedies, Gates recommended a specific course of action:

The first and most important, as it seems to me, is to found a great college, ultimately to be a University, in Chicago. We need in Chicago an institution with an endowment of several millions with buildings, library, and other appliances equal to any on the continent; an institution commanding the services of the ablest scientific culture, and aiming to counteract the western tendency to a merely superficial and utilitarian education . . . . Between the Allegheny and the Rocky Mountains there is not to be found another city in which such an institution as we need could be established or if established could be maintained and enlarged, or if maintained could achieve wide influence or retain supremacy among us.

Thomas W. Goodspeed

Goodspeed promptly sent a copy of this address to Harper, hinting that the latter might wish to pass it on to Rockefeller. At the December meeting of the Education Society in Washington, Gates again read his paper, and the board passed a resolution declaring that the establishment of a Baptist institution of higher learning in Chicago was "an immediate and imperative necessity." Thus the denomination, through this agency, had spoken officially. What was now required

to turn expectation into reality were money and leadership. Would Rockefeller accept the Chicago plan as the will of the denomination, and would Harper agree to organize an institution such as Gates had described?

These delicate and promising negotiations were interrupted temporarily when, four days into the new year of 1889, Gates received a letter from Morehouse informing him that Harper "has peremptorily declined to take the presidency of the proposed University of Chicago and says he has told Mr. Rockefeller so. The reasons for this you will know in due time if not now . . . . There have been some new developments." What had happened was that a few days earlier, during the Christmas recess, Strong had read through the notes his daughter had taken in Harper's class at Vassar. Grave doubts arising in his mind as to the orthodoxy of his rival from Yale, he drafted a letter to Harper asking him to explain questionable doctrinal points. Strong sent a copy of this letter to Rockefeller, an action interpreted by the proponents of the Chicago university as an attempt to frustrate their enterprise.

Deeply disturbed, Harper sought to disassociate himself from the Chicago plan in order not to compromise it. His withdrawal was particularly serious since Gates and the others had expected that Rockefeller, given the action of the Education Society, would seize the initiative toward establishing the university. In fact, Rockefeller seemed more reticent than ever. Morehouse believed that if Harper had declared his willingness to accept the presidency of the proposed university, Rockefeller would have responded immediately:

I am convinced in my own mind that Mr. Rockefeller is waiting for the right man to be found for the presidency of the institution. He takes great stock in men. I believe if Harper would have accepted a month ago that Mr. Rockefeller's decision would have been given then; but he has taken himself out of the field and as nobody else is conspicuous for the place I am apprehensive that Mr. Rockefeller will wait until the right man is found. If therefore my theory is correct, and his decision hinges upon a man it may be months before he will decide.

Gates discerned another possible reason for Rockefeller's reluctance: his preference for an undergraduate college in Chicago instead of a full-fledged university. On January 13, Gates wrote a long letter to Rockefeller proposing that the Society establish a strong college in Chicago. If this project were successful, then the question of a university could be taken up. Now that he had declined to be a candidate for the presidency, Harper along with Goodspeed approved the plan. Rockefeller, too, was evidently impressed with the approach; he asked Morehouse and Gates to lunch with him on January 16 to discuss the details in person. The day before this meeting, Rockefeller sent a letter to Harper which said, in part:

So many claims have pressed upon me, I have not really needed a University to absorb my surplus . . . Of late I had rather come to feel that if Chicago could get a College, and leave the question of a University until a later date, that this would be more likely to be accomplished.

It was now time for the Education Society to draw up a definite plan. In February, Gates appointed nine leading educators, including Harper and Morehouse, to a "Committee of Inquiry on the Proposed Institution of Learning in Chicago." Before appointing the committee, Gates inquired of Rockefeller whether such a group might prove an "embarrassment" to Rockefeller's own plans; on the contrary, Rockefeller replied, anything he might do for Chicago he preferred to do through the Society. The committee held meetings through the spring of 1889 and prepared a report to be delivered at the annual meeting of the Education Society in May.

To prevent further complications, steps were taken to reassure Strong. Harper's reply to Strong's queries and the testimony of Goodspeed and Northrup had effectively reaffirmed Harper's doctrinal soundness; if anything, Strong's intervention earlier in the year may have weakened his own position with Rockefeller. Yet Strong's commitment to the project for the New York graduate school posed a potential threat to Chicago. Attempts were made by Harper, Gates, and Goodspeed to persuade him that what was proposed for Chicago was in no sense a rival to his own dream.

As the months of deliberation and discussion neared an end, the movement toward decision picked up speed. The report of the Committee of Inquiry recommended that the sum of $1 million be raised to establish the new institution in Chicago. On May 7, Harper wrote to Goodspeed of another visit Rockefeller had paid to him at Vassar:

He said at least a dozen times: "The next thing for us to do, and the correct thing for us to do is to establish a college at Chicago." He expressed himself as satisfied with the report of the committee in nearly every detail. He has only one or two changes which he expects to make, and that he is going to take hold of the Chicago University is as certain as that there is a God in heaven. I feel greatly encouraged.

Both the Society and Rockefeller had spoken of a college, but Harper was clearly once again thinking of a more ambitious enterprise.

A few days before the May meeting of the Education Society, Gates met with Rockefeller at his New York office. There he secured a pledge of $600,000 toward the establishment of the new "college" at Chicago. At the meeting of the Society, Gates withheld the announcement of the pledge, at Rockefeller's request, until the

Frederick T. Gates

*On following pages:
John D. Rockefeller's pledge to contribute $600,000 toward the establishment of the University, 1889*

26 Broadway,
New York.

May 15th 1889.

Rev. Fred T. Gates, Cor. Sec'y,

American Baptist Education Society.

My dear Sir:

I will contribute six hundred thousand dollars, ($600.000#) toward an endowment fund for a college to be established at Chicago, the income only of which may be used for current expenses, but not for land, buildings or repairs, providing four hundred thousand dollars, ($400.000#) more is pledged by good and responsible parties, satisfactory to the Board of the American Baptist Education Society and myself, on or before June 1st 1890; said four hundred thousand dollars, or as much of it as shall be required,

26 Broadway,
New York.

to be used for the purpose of purchasing land and erecting buildings, the remainder of the same to be added to the above six hundred thousand dollars, as endowment.

I will pay the same to the American Baptist Education Society in five years, beginning within ninety days after completion of the subscription as above, and pay five per cent. each ninety days thereafter until all is paid; providing not less than a proportionate amount is so paid by the other subscribers to the four hundred thousand dollars; otherwise this pledge to be null and void.

Yours, very truly,

Jno. D. Rockefeller.

Society had committed itself to raise the necessary funds to proceed with the plan.

The decision made, there remained a year of hard work to raise the matching amount of $400,000 stipulated by Rockefeller's gift. Gates and Goodspeed devoted their full energies to the campaign. Within two months almost $250,000 was pledged by the Baptists of Chicago. An additional $50,000 came from Baptist congregations outside the city, many of which had at first looked on the move to establish a school in Chicago as a purely local concern. Equally gratifying was the response of the leadership of Chicago's non-Baptist community. With the enthusiastic help of men such as Charles L. Hutchinson, Martin A. Ryerson, Marshall Field, E. B. Felsenthal, and others, the rest of the needed sum was secured.

John D. Rockefeller

Harper's Plan

The University's Articles of Incorporation were formally adopted on June 18, 1890. They committed the institution to sexual equality, to undergraduate and graduate education, and, significantly, considering the intention to found a Baptist school, to an atmosphere of nonsectarianism. Although two-thirds of the trustees and the president were to be Baptists (this specification was later amended), "no other religious test or particular religious profession shall ever be held as a requisite for election to said board, or for admission to said University, or to any department belonging thereto . . . or for election to any professorship." Gates called this "a very broad charter."

At the same time, the Board of Trustees was selected. Rockefeller declined to serve, and E. Nelson Blake, a prominent local Baptist, soon resigned the chairmanship in favor of Martin Ryerson. Three swampy blocks fronting the Midway Plaisance were acquired from the Chicago retailer Marshall Field, giving the University a home in Hyde Park, a middle-class community seven miles south of downtown, which had been annexed by the city of Chicago in 1889.

After all this rapid accomplishment, what proved to be time-consuming was the delicate task of persuading Harper to accept the presidency. Harper was the only candidate seriously considered by the Board. His reputation unscathed by the questions asked by Strong, Harper was nevertheless troubled by doubt as to whether he could be both president of a Baptist institution, whether a university or a college, and a critical scholar of the scriptures. At the age of thirty-two, holding two major professorships at Yale, Harper had achieved an enviable position in the academic world. His friends in New Haven told him he would be a fool to accept the presidency; his friends in Chicago told him he must. Goodspeed wrote: "No other man has been thought of . . . . You are the choice of the denomination." Harper replied with some coyness:

E. Nelson Blake

On opposite page: William Rainey Harper, 1903

The letters continue to be received. I think I shall have to preserve them and bind them in a separate file. Whether I accept the position or not it will be pleasant to look back to these letters and to read them. The statements in your letter are, I am afraid, too strong, but I am ready to admit that the case is a serious one. I am laboring on three distinct points; one or two of them I think I can get into shape, but the third is a stickler. It does not seem possible to do what ought to be done, what the denomination will expect, with the money we have in hand. There must in someway be an assurance of an additional million. How this is to be obtained, or where, is the question. If Mr. R. is dead in earnest, possibly the case will not be so difficult as we may think.

As this letter indicated, Harper remained insistent on enlarging the work of the University; the result was seen in a message Rockefeller sent to the Board ten days after the University was legally incorporated. He was willing to contribute $800,000 to endow non-professional graduate work, $100,000 for the theological endowment, and $100,000 for theological buildings. Two days after the receipt of Rockefeller's letter, the Board unanimously elected Harper President of the University. He requested six months to consider. In a note on a letter written to Morehouse, Harper indicated that his acceptance would be contingent on the Board's acceptance of his plan for the institution: "I have a plan for the organization of the University which will revolutionize College and University work in this country. It is 'bran splinter new,' and yet as solid as the ancient hills."

Harper's plan was set forth in six *Official Bulletins,* which appeared between January 1891 and May 1982. *Official Bulletin* No. 1 set forth the basic structure of the University, which was taken up in detail in the remaining five bulletins. Harper conceived of a University with three main divisions: (1) The University proper would include the Graduate Schools and Colleges of Arts, Literature, and Science, the Professional Schools, preparatory academies such as the one at Morgan Park, and any affiliated schools, which would be independent but cooperating institutions; (2) The University Extension Division would offer lectures and courses for the working men and women of Chicago and correspondence courses for those at a distance from the city; and (3) The University Publication Work was to be responsible for the printing of University announcements and scholarly books and journals. Yet another innovation under Harper's plan was an academic year divided into four quarters with a convocation held each quarter. Through the quarter system, Harper wrote in his first annual report, "The student will receive his diploma, not because a certain number of years have passed and a certain day in June arrived, but because his work is finished."

The *Official Bulletins* presented Harper's vision for Chicago.

Martin A. Ryerson

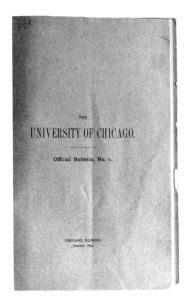

Official Bulletin *No. 1*

Articles of Incorporation, 1890

On February 16, 1891, he formally accepted appointment as the University's first President. Now began the work of transforming the sketch into actuality. Henry Ives Cobb, chosen as University Architect, drew up a master plan of the campus, and work began on the first buildings. A drive was started to raise an additional $1 million for the building program. At first the building drive went slowly, and Harper occasionally voiced despair to Gates:

I ought not to write you this morning. I am not in a good mood. I do not suppose I ought to betray the mood in which I am, but I am accustomed to speak out what I feel and how I feel. . . . The pressure here in Chicago for the World's Fair, the World's Fair Memorial, the Art Institute and a thousand other things is tremendous. I ought not to be discouraged; I am not; and yet, a sort of general feeling of despair in reference to the whole situation, its difficulties and embarrassments seems to be taking possession of me.

A breakthrough came when Silas Cobb (not related to the architect) gave the University $150,000. Cobb Hall, still a center of undergraduate instruction, was the first building erected on the campus. In the following months, gifts for buildings were received from Sidney Kent, Martin Ryerson, Mrs. Elizabeth Kelly, Mrs. Nancy A. Foster, George Walker, and others.

Finding scholars for the classrooms was Harper's greatest concern in those first months. Determined that the University should begin with a faculty composed of the leading scholars in every academic field, he knew what he was looking for:

It is only a man who has made investigation who can teach others to investigate. . . . Promotion of younger men in the department will depend more largely upon the results of their work as investigators than upon the efficiency of their teaching, although the latter will by no means be overlooked. In other words it is proposed in this institution to make the work of investigation primary, the work of giving instruction secondary.

Harper's resourcefulness in persuading first-rate scholars to move to Chicago was to become legendary. Inexorably persistent in pursuit, he was adroit in using Rockefeller's money to offer academic salaries far above the norm of the times. In a letter to Goodspeed in 1892, for example, Harper reported on the progress of his attempts to lure Ernest DeWitt Burton from the Newton Theological Institution, as well as the chemist Ira Remsen from Johns Hopkins:

As I telegraphed you yesterday, Burton has declined. He has just telegraphed me that he cannot free himself from the obligations that seem to rest upon him there. What we shall do now is a mystery. . . . I can think of absolutely no one to put in this chair. . . . Remsen is in great trouble. I think he will come, but he has not yet decided. They are moving heaven and earth to keep him at Baltimore. Unfortunately a full announcement of the fact appeared in the daily papers at Baltimore on

Henry Ives Cobb

the morning of my arrival. It is not altogether a pleasant task to be lecturing in the University and trying to take away one of its professors at the same time.

Burton finally decided to accept Harper's offer; Remsen, on the other hand, remained at Hopkins. The trustees there had outwitted Harper by electing the chemist president of that institution.

Henry Ives Cobb's proposed master plan for the University, 1893

Site of the University

View of campus from World's Columbian
Exposition Ferris Wheel, 1893

The First Year

My dear Miss Talbot:

I hope you will turn a kind ear toward Mr. Harper's propositions. We are going in time—not instantly—to have a great University in Chicago, and it seems to me it might well be an attractive idea to you [to] help shape its policy, at the outset, in some very important lines. And you mustn't think of "missionary work," either. Chicago is not what the average reader of Eastern newspapers imagines. I went out, on my first visit, with full New England prejudice; but I have come to see how greatly likeable the place is, and am already strongly attached to a number of people. There is life and happiness in Chicago.

Sincerely yours,
W. G. Hale

The summer of 1892 was a time of great expectation for those who had accepted the "call" and a period of hectic activity for those preparing for the opening of the University. Even the more intrepid such as Marion Talbot, who had come to Chicago from Wellesley to become Dean of Women in the University Colleges and Assistant Professor of Sanitary Science, felt some apprehension.

President Harper filled notebooks with lists of projects to be undertaken, arrangements to be made, tasks to be completed. Terse entries enumerated faculty who had accepted, appointments yet to be confirmed, salaries and titles, and course assignments. The brevity and variety of the notes captured the breakneck pace of the summer's work: "Telephone Stagg for plans; Cheaper room for women; Dougherty of Peoria; Von Holst—Thatcher."

Preparatory activities were not restricted to the administrative officers. During the summer, a group of students-to-be organized the first campus newspaper, the *University of Chicago Weekly*. The first issue contained articles by professors, a grandiloquent editorial, and essential information for the entering student:

Marion Talbot

Alice Freeman Palmer

By mutual agreement between all the faculty and officers of the University now on hand, the uniform appellation of "Mr." has been adopted in mutual intercourse, thus doing away with all doubts and mistakes as to the proper title of any man connected with the institution.

Meanwhile, pressure intensified to ensure that the initial buildings—Cobb Lecture Hall and the three graduate dormitories later named Gates, Blake, and Goodspeed—would be ready for the October 1 opening. Additional space being needed, the Trustees rented several buildings in the neighborhood for temporary classrooms and living quarters. Some faculty and women students were assigned to the Hotel Beatrice. Dean Talbot, writing to her parents in Boston, described the hotel and the campus buildings as they appeared in late September:

We arrived at Hyde Park at 4:30 P.M. Mrs. Palmer [Alice Freeman Palmer, Dean of Women], Prof. Hale and I, were met by Mr. Laughlin, who waved at us the first number of the *University of Chicago Weekly*. Isn't it like this great, rushing city, to have a student publication out a week before the institution opens its doors? Prof. Laughlin took us to the Hotel Vendome where we left our bags and bundles and there went with all speed to have a glimpse of "The Beatrice." As we turned from Monroe Ave. [renamed Dorchester] into 57th Street we beheld my future abode, a six story structure in the middle of a block, towering way up over the scattered cottages round about it. Inside all was confusion. The house, with its twelve apartments, was finished, but the rooms and halls were full of rubbish. We did not linger long, but hurried on to the University to see our academic home. Cobb Hall to be used this year by graduate students, was in even worse condition for it was far from completion. We were much impressed however with its quiet strength and beauty as we looked at it across the rough field and from the hole in the ground Mr. Laughlin asked us to imagine as his house. We made our way in the twilight through the corridors, scrambling over piles of lumber and shavings and nearly falling thro the holes in the landings where loose boards served as treads. It all looked very promising, but more so for next year than for next month. However, this is Chicago we thought.

Cobb Hall construction

On Saturday, October 1, 1892, the work of the University began. The decision was made to forego opening ceremonies; class began that morning as if the University had been in session for some time. At 12:30 P.M. a chapel service took place in the Cobb Hall assembly room. The service was simple: prayer, scripture reading, and hymns.

At 4:30 P.M. the faculty held its first meeting. The University Recorder, Charles R. Henderson, was so overcome by the sense of occasion that he neglected to take minutes. The official minutes were later compiled from notes taken by Dean Talbot. In his opening remarks President Harper stated that the question before the faculty was how to become one in spirit, if not necessarily one in opinion. Whether to admit secret societies to the University was the first item of business placed before the faculty. The mechanics of the weekly bulletins were explained, and the examiner announced the number of students who had matriculated on the first day: 126 enrolled in the Graduate Schools, 85 upperclassmen and 85 freshmen in the College, 61 special students, and 153 enrolled in the Divinity School for a total of 510. The meeting adjourned after the President expressed the hope that the first two years of the undergraduate program would eventually be transferred to a separate campus so that the "higher work [i.e., graduate study] be given all our strength on this campus."

Despite the absence of tradition and amenities, a pattern of campus life quickly established itself. The flavor of the first days was caught in the diary entries of Demia Butler from Indianapolis, who was in the freshman class:

October 17, 1892 — In the afternoon Mrs. Palmer addressed the women of the colleges. She spoke of the great advantages of college life, and of college life in the midst of a great progressive city, urging the students to make the most of their advantages in musical and artistic matters; and to cherish well and thoughtfully the strengthening companionships of student life. In the evening the Beatrice gathered in the reception to hear Mr. Stagg talk on Foot Ball.

He drew the "field" on a sheet of paper and hung it on the wall, marking the positions of the men with dots and crosses. He explained the different movements very clearly. After he told us of the great physical, mental, and moral strength the game demanded and what a fine discipline it is in all three things we were prepared to enjoy it with greater zest than ever.

October 31 — A dozen or more of the Beatrice girls arranged for a Hallow e'vn party. We sent out invitations to the rest of the household, and one outsider, Mr. Stagg. The receiving committee wore the Oxford caps made of white paper and yellow pasteboards, and draped sheets like Oxford gowns. The guests wore their sheets and pillow cases as they chose, and many of them came masked. As Professor Stagg was draped in a sheet in the reception room Dr. Nordell remarked, noting the but half-completed condition of the draping over the shoulders and back — "Half-back." Bess Messick spoke up, "No tonight he is centre rush" — He was the only unmarried man invited. The Dining hall was draped with yellow; the lights turned low, and the Jack'O Lanterns shed but a dim light over the white robed figures. We played games and ate candy and chestnuts for a while, then Dr. Nordell read us Burns' "Tam o' Shanter." Mr. Stagg complied with our request to "give us his 'Little Drama.'" It was very funny indeed! He is a man of widely varied talents. His "encore" was a short but exceedingly laughable song. Then more games, and bobbing for apples, and it was time to re-arrange the dining room, and set the tables — for the maids had gone and we had been granted the use of the hall upon condition that we leave it ready for breakfast. It was great fun.

The relationship between the campus community and the city was strong from the beginning. The support that Chicagoans gave to the first fundraising drive exceeded expectations. Local residents

The Midway with the Ferris Wheel
(at right: Foster Hall under construction)

Marion Talbot's invitation to the Opening
Ceremonies of the World's Columbian Exposition

*Mrs. John J. Glessner (sixth from left on balcony)
and her Monday Morning Reading Class*

*The heads of the women's residences, 1895. Left to right:
Myra Reynolds, Marion Talbot, Elizabeth Wallace*

found ways to make the faculty and students feel at home. Mrs. John J. Glessner organized a Monday Morning Reading Class, which gave faculty wives an opportunity to meet her friends in her famous house at 1800 Prairie Avenue. To provide financial aid to needy students, Mrs. Glessner joined with other friends of the University to establish the Students' Fund Society. This was one way, Mrs. Glessner wrote to President Harper, "for the city people, who are not able to give large sums, to make themselves a part of the University."

If there were those among the academic community who tried to resist the lure of the "great progressive city," then the dedication ceremonies of the World's Columbian Exposition late in October forcibly brought them face to face with the city and, indeed, the world. Dean Talbot described the stirring occasion to her parents:

Here I am one of 125,000 guests invited to take part in the opening exercises of this stupendous undertaking. . . . The proportions of the hall [Manufacturers' Building] are beautiful and it is very hard to estimate the distances. We seem to be a little one side of the middle in both directions. The tremendous chorus (5,000) is rehearsing at one end and we hear comparatively little except during the drum and cymbal passages.

When the Exposition opened to visitors the next summer, students and faculty alike encountered exhibits of exotic life stretched along the Midway Plaisance as the buildings of the University continued to rise across the street. The historian Henry Adams found the Exposition an unnervingly impressive experience. "Education ran riot at Chicago," he noted in his book, *The Education of Henry Adams*. "Chicago was the first expression of American thought as a unity; one must start there." For many who came to the University in 1892, the sweep of the Columbian Exposition may well have symbolized the aspiration of the builders of the University. Academic life had to be organized in spite of the limited resources, but the faculty and students had gathered and the work of the University had begun.

Members of the Geology Department: front row left, Rollin D. Salisbury; front row center, Thomas C. Chamberlin

The Faculty

The college, which had been established with the provision that expansion would follow as resources permitted, had, through Harper's vision, become a university. The first priority in Harper's mind was to explore the possibility of organizing knowledge in new ways through active research and by training future scholars. "It is agreed by all that our first work is graduate work," he wrote.

Many joined the faculty out of a conviction that the University would provide an opportunity to organize scholarly disciplines unencumbered by prevailing academic convention. Typical of such recruits was George Herbert Mead, soon to become one of the major American theorists of social philosophy and psychology. Mead joined the faculty in 1894; his work marked a turning away from speculative philosophies of the nineteenth century toward a philosophy rooted in empirical investigation. Two years before he joined the faculty, Mead argued that scholarship should not be cloistered from the real world; rather, a university should be organized "so that it can direct action" in various fields of investigation. Regarding his research, Mead wrote, "I hope myself shortly to start up mothers' clubs and psychological societies which will study the young child and the mental image." A similar sentiment was expressed by Albion W. Small, who had resigned the presidency of Colby College to organize the Department of Sociology, the first such department in the country. Small called upon scholars to study and comment on everyday life "in concrete form," asking, "What is the use of thinking, if it is not in the last analysis, a part of the world's real doing?"

Hermann von Holst, a German authority on the U.S. Constitution who joined the first faculty, wrote frequently on current political affairs. One issue on which the historian commented was the 1894 Pullman strike. He was asked to write an article on the strike for the *Journal of Political Economy*. In making the request, J. Laurence Laughlin, Head Professor of Political Economy, wrote von Holst:

Hermann von Holst

There never was a time when we more needed a ringing article on the governmental questions arising from the conditions produced by strikers and labor organizations. . . . The effect of Altgeld's and Debs' proclamations should be met, and Cleveland supported; the constitutionality of the questions clearly discussed; the effect of this looseness of obedience to law, which seems to be growing, on democracy, etc., etc. This only by way of hint. You can lean as much as you like to the economic side; but "load your gun for bear." I hope you will not find it in your heart to decline this call of duty.

Von Holst's article "Are We Awakened?" appeared in September 1894 and supported the action of the federal government. In other matters, von Holst took positions that were not so generally popular. He deplored the Spanish-American War and the annexation of Hawaii, with the result that some segments of the press denounced him as a foreign traitor.

William Vaughn Moody

When Laughlin came to the University to organize the Department of Political Economy, he brought with him a protégé whose task it became to edit the *Journal of Political Economy*. Despite the fact that Laughlin and his younger colleague, Thorstein Veblen, held divergent economic views, the relationship was one of cordiality and mutual respect. From the student's point of view, the opportunity to study with two such original economists proved to be enormously stimulating. The essayist Stephen Leacock, who received his Ph.D. in economics in 1903, sketched this profile of Veblen in his "Recollections of the University of Chicago":

I took many lectures from Thorstein Veblen and was deeply impressed by him. He had no manner, no voice, no art. He lectured into his lap with his eyes on his waistcoat. But he would every now and then drop a phrase with a literary value to it beyond the common reach. In the first lecture I heard, he happened to say, "Hume, of course, aspired to be an intellectual tough." That got me, and kept me; the art of words is almost better than truth, isn't it.

Albert A. Michelson

In his influential book, *The Theory of the Leisure Class*, Veblen drew upon his Chicago experience for some of his more trenchant comments on collegiate Gothic architecture, traditional academic regalia, and the popularity of sports.

The core of the Department of English Language and Literature was a number of young men who had known one another, and in some cases worked together, at Harvard. The first to arrive at the University was Robert Herrick, an aspiring novelist. Shortly thereafter, Herrick was joined by Robert Morss Lovett, William Vaughn Moody, and in 1898, by John Matthews Manly, who was Chairman of the department for almost four decades. Much of the literary criticism at the end of the nineteenth century tended to base critical judgments on moral preconceptions, or to isolate literary works from their historical and social context. Manly and his colleagues articulated an approach to literature that emphasized the historical development of literary forms and works. "The main things we need to do, it seems to me," Manly wrote to Lovett in 1898:

are to provide a good series of courses requiring wide reading and covering the field of English literary history systematically and somewhat in detail; and in general to transfer the emphasis of our work from systems of aesthetics and ethics to the more literary study of literature.

If Manly represented a new breed of literary scholar, Moody and Herrick applied themselves primarily to the task of creating imaginative literature. During his lifetime Moody was considered one of America's leading poets, and, near the end of his short life, the success of his prose plays, *The Great Divide* and *The Faithhealer*, placed him in the front ranks of contemporary dramatists. For Herrick, the city of Chicago provided a major stimulus for his fiction. The austere New Englander found his voice as an urban realist. As he noted in one of his autobiographical manuscripts:

The University of Chicago was in its early years less formally academic, less narrow, less inhibiting to the individual than the more conventional eastern institutions. Being situated in what is thought to be the most American of all our centres, it is impossible for it to maintain a watertight compartment of purely academic life. One inevitably felt the life of the community as is revealed in my early novels . . .

Herrick described the sharp contrasts between the lives of the wealthy and the poor, who frequently lived in close physical proximity. He portrayed the effects of urban life on the human spirit and was particularly attuned to the subtle, and often corrupting, effects of urban "opportunity" on the educated and professional classes.

During these formative years, the science departments were funded by a gift from the estate of William Ogden, who had been an active trustee of the "old" University of Chicago. As initially organized, the Ogden (Graduate) School of Science included the Departments of Physics, Chemistry, Geology, Astronomy, Mathematics, and Biology—the last-named subsequently subdivided into Zoology, Botany, Anatomy, Neurology, and Physiology.

When Albert A. Michelson came to the University, he was already famous for the Michelson-Morley experiment of 1887, which investigated the effects of relative motion on the velocity of light. The result of this experiment proved the velocity of light to be a constant, a cornerstone of the theory of relativity. During the 1892–93 academic year, Michelson traveled in Europe, purchasing equipment

Robert Herrick

Thorstein Veblen

On following pages: The Seventh Convocation, July 2, 1894. Albert A. Michelson delivering the convocation address on "Light Waves and their Use." President Harper is seated directly behind Michelson. At the end of the second row, right to left, are John Dewey, William Gardner Hale, and J. Laurence Laughlin.

and instruments. The following year the first classes were held in Ryerson Physical Laboratory.

A passage in a letter from Michelson to Harper gives some idea of how close an interest the President was assumed to take in the progress of research:

The science of Spectroscopy has accomplished a number of remarkable feats within the past decade and there appears every reason to expect that an improvement in the essential element of the Spectroscope—that is, the "grating"—will be followed by a corresponding unfolding of hitherto hidden secrets of Nature's laboratory. It is with the manufacture and improvement of such "diffraction grating" that I am chiefly occupied. The process consists in the ruling of exceedingly fine lines (with a diamond point) upon an optically true metal surface—the difficulty to be overcome being the extraordinary accuracy required in the spacing of these lines. This is largely determined by the accuracy of a precision screw—which I am having constructed in our workshop. Thus far difficulties have arisen on account of imperfections of screwcutting machinery. These are now in a fair way to being overcome, and I hope to obtain encouraging results within a few months.

In 1907, Michelson was awarded the Nobel Prize in Physics—the first American so honored—for, in the words of the citation, "his precision optical instruments and the spectroscopic and meteorological investigations conducted therewith."

Like Michelson, John U. Nef, Sr., the distinguished chemist, was one of seven faculty members who came to Chicago following an academic dispute at Clark University. Trained in Germany, Nef had been much impressed with the scientific institutes there, which permitted research to be carried on apart from teaching. Research institutes after the German pattern were as yet unknown in the United States, and it was unlikely that a scientist in an academic context could avoid all teaching responsibilities. In 1894, when the Department of Chemistry was asked to initiate an undergraduate course, Nef wrote to the president of Clark, G. Stanley Hall, asking if it were possible for him to return to Clark.

Nef decided to stay at Chicago, but throughout his career he sought to free research work from those areas of academic responsibility that, he felt, weakened it. One of his innovations was to appoint a recent Ph.D. graduate as his research assistant, thereby initiating the postdoctoral research fellowship. In a memorandum prepared for the Committee on Research of the Ogden School of Science, Nef declared firmly, "The most precious and vital factor in a University is the man, and in that connection discrimination in regard to the relative value of men must be exercised. The men—not the bricks—are the foundation of a University."

John U. Nef, Sr., and his son John U. Nef, Jr.

Just as Harper had filled all the faculty positions allotted to the sciences, he was faced with a prospect he found irresistible: Thomas C. Chamberlin, the eminent geologist. As president of the University of Wisconsin, Chamberlin had transformed a midwestern college into a university with a growing reputation; now he wished to return to teaching. He accepted the invitation to come to Chicago to organize the Department of Geology, bringing with him his associate Rollin D. Salisbury as Professor of Geographic Geology (the Department of Geography, the first of its kind, was organized in 1903 with Salisbury as Chairman). One of Chamberlin's initial concerns was the creation of a departmental publication, the *Journal of Geology*. In a letter written to Salisbury while both were still at Madison, he discussed one feature of the proposed journal which would render it more useful to the teacher:

Studies for Students . . . intended to furnish a place for analytical and critical discussions that would be deemed elementary and perhaps bordering on
the offensive addressed to professional geologists (however much they may need
them) but which would be perfectly appropriate in a University publication
intended to subserve the double purpose of teaching and original publications.
These analytical studies would be anticipatory of the textbooks and be a means
by which we could get them before geologists for criticism and emendation
and before students for trial and adaptation.

Chicago Philosophy Club, ca. 1896

In some cases scientific research was carried on away from the University. In 1902, Howard Taylor Ricketts joined the faculty as an Associate Professor in the Department of Pathology and Bacteriology. He soon became interested in investigating the causes of Rocky Mountain Spotted Fever. Aided by funds from the American Medical Association, the Montana State Board of Health, and the University, Ricketts conducted extensive field explorations, collecting data, which he brought back to the laboratories at the University for detailed analysis. In June 1907, he wrote to Dr. Ludwig Hektoen, head of the Department of Pathology and Bacteriology, about his work:

I sent the message to you yesterday because I thought we had demonstrated infected ticks in nature in two instances and wanted to get an avenue of speedy publication in case we could satisfy ourselves that we were correct. Fortunately or unfortunately we have found since yesterday that one of the supposed positive tests didn't hold water. The visceral changes were perfectly typical, but cultures and the inoculation of other guinea-pigs from the dead one showed it to be at least a complicated case, hence not reliable . . . . The point is essential before the tick theory can be accepted unreservedly, and this phase of the work has taken more of my time than any other one thing.

As it turned out, the experiments of 1907 fully confirmed the wood-tick as the carrier of Rocky Mountain Spotted Fever. Three years later, while carrying on a similar inquiry into the causes of typhus, Ricketts contracted and later died from the then-fatal disease.

Howard Taylor Ricketts

*The University Express, travelling
from 57th Street Station on its way
to Ryerson Physical Laboratory*

The Early College

The initial undergraduate program at the University was outlined in the *Official Bulletin* No. 2 of April 1891. Harper viewed the traditional four-year undergraduate course as better divided into two divisions, with the freshman and sophomore years treated as really an extension of secondary education. The first two years were called the Academic College (a name later changed to the Junior College). According to Harper, "The work of the first two years partakes largely of the Academic character. The regulations must still be strict. The scope of election is limited."

The last two years, at first known as the University College, later the Senior College, were to anticipate graduate work. Harper wrote,

The close of the second year marks the beginning of a new period. . . . The student begins to specialize and in many cases may to advantage select subjects which will bear directly or indirectly upon the work of his chosen calling. . . . The student gradually changes from the College atmosphere to that of the University. Different motives incite him to work.

While Harper hoped that the first two years of undergraduate instruction might be carried on away from the main campus, it remained entirely on the Quadrangles. As the focal point of the collegiate experience, the Junior College became the battleground for two volatile issues during the Harper years. The first led to heated confrontation between the sciences and the humanities; the second between the sexes.

The "Latin Question" erupted in 1892 and remained alive for a decade. The major antagonists were the geologist Thomas Chamberlin and the classicist William Gardner Hale. The controversy began when Chamberlin proposed that Junior College students be permitted to elect a modern language in place of Latin. This suggestion outraged the classicists, who declared that Latin was the foundation of the curriculum and essential to a liberal education.

Harold Swift as "Filippo" during his freshman year, 1904. Swift was the first alumnus elected to the Board of Trustees, serving from 1914 until his death in 1962.

Most of the scientists on the faculty shared Chamberlin's view, perceiving the issue not only as science versus the humanities, but as specialization versus liberal education. Sensitivities aroused by the dispute were revealed when Harper asked Chamberlin to comment on plans for the first meeting of the University Congregation, an advisory body to the University administration. After criticizing the draft of the opening ceremonies as too elaborate, Chamberlin denounced "the old scholasticism," whose indifference or opposition to modern science galled him:

In addition to the general objections, the singing of the Latin hymn is especially distasteful to some of us, because of the regrettable attitude of some of the advocates of Latin toward the free development of the science courses. To some of us Latin has come, as a result of this, to stand for much the same thing in the scholarly world that Romanism does in the ecclesiastical world, and this is likely to grow in intensity so long as the existing intolerant attitude is maintained and its ill effects continue to be felt. The introduction, therefore, of a special feature that particularly commemorates the attitude of the old scholasticism, from whose tyrannies we are not yet escaped, is especially distasteful in a general assembly . . . .

In 1905, Latin became an elective for those enrolled in the bachelor of science course of study.

The second issue—"segregation," as it was called—arose in 1900. In its charter the University had pledged to provide equal educational opportunities for both men and women. When the University opened its doors in 1892, the proportion of women students was small. However, by the turn of the century there were almost as many women matriculating as men.

In 1900, a suggestion was made that better educational results could be achieved in the Junior College if men and women were taught separately. The reasoning behind this was obscure: some felt that the women students distracted the men; others thought that studying with men might "defeminize" women. The matter came to a head in 1902 when the University was considering a gift of over $1 million to build a separate educational facility for Junior College women. Several Trustees and faculty members, attempting to separate the question of the potential gift from the educational issues, sought opinions both pro and con from educators around the country. Jenkin Lloyd Jones, a Unitarian cleric and founder of the Abraham Lincoln Center in Chicago, wrote to Board member Charles L. Hutchinson:

However much the management may desire to the contrary, this proposed "segregation" will be regarded, and rightly so, as the most serious blow that co-education has ever received in America at the hand of any institution of learning . . . . The disproportion of sexes is not peculiar to the U. of C. It runs through all the higher interests of life—church, philanthropy and reform. The remedy

Pearl Hood and Ruth Cohen outside
a women's residence hall, 1901

Miss Kimball and Miss Chamberlin
in front of a women's residence hall,
ca. 1900

Mandolin, Banjo, and Guitar Club, 1895

does not come by killing off or by heading off the women, but by bringing up the masculine reserve. Let us eliminate the crudeness, coarseness and selfishness out of our boys and then they will not be ashamed when found in competition with their sisters and they will not be rude when in their presence.

Such sentiments notwithstanding, the policy of segregation of men and women students in the Junior College was adopted in 1902, and a temporary building, Lexington Hall, was erected to provide classrooms for the women students. This arrangement soon proved untenable, and, although not officially repudiated, segregation by gender ceased to be practiced within a short time.

Undergraduate activities outside the classroom were highly conventional; the students of the new university seemed determined to establish all those aspects of college life that were considered traditional. Fraternities were admitted to the campus, but, in the face of Dean Talbot's disapproval, sororities were not. Instead, "Women's Clubs" were organized and space provided for them in University buildings. Some groups reflected the diverse origins of the student body: the Southern Club, the Scandinavian Club, the Japanese Club, and for those from any other foreign land, the Cosmopolitan Club. Secret societies, debating clubs, musical societies, social gatherings, and athletic events varied the academic round. The ancestor of the modern coffee shop, "The Shanty," had been a refreshment stand at the Columbian Exposition; it was moved to the corner of the athletic field where it provided coffee, food, and conversation.

The University had two student newspapers, the *Weekly* and the *University News*, but the latter ceased publication in 1893. Except for the brave attempt of a Divinity School student to start a publication

*Football team with player-coach Amos
Alonzo Stagg holding ball, 1892*

Sideline pass, 1904

called the *University Arena* (issue one was also the last), student newspapers remained in the preserve of the undergraduates. A newspaper titled the *Maroon* appeared as early as the academic year 1895–96. And, in 1901, when the *Weekly* was still flourishing, a new publication was founded called the *Daily Maroon*. The two newspapers continued their daily and weekly coverage until 1902, when the *Weekly* ceased publication.

Athletic competition was a major source of excitement on campus, with the greatest share of attention being directed toward the football team. When Bartlett Gymnasium was dedicated in 1904, its stained-glass window and lobby mural depicting knightly combat attempted to suggest the lineage of athletic contests. The same year a fund was established to purchase chimes for Mitchell Tower. When making his contribution, Amos Alonzo Stagg wrote to President Harper:

I was greatly depressed and worried by the spirit shown by our team in the Thanksgiving Day contest, and in casting about for possible helpful things, my mind went back to my own college days at Yale. The sweet chimes of Battell Chapel had always been an inspiration to me, and I recalled the many many times during the period of my training that the cheery, hopeful ten o'clock chime had led me to fall asleep with a quiet determination for a greater devotion to duty and to my ideals. The thought came to me and filled me with deepest satisfaction. "Why not have a good night chime for our own athletes" — to let its sweet cadence have a last word with them before they fell asleep; to speak to them of love and loyalty and sacrifice for their University, and of hope and inspiration and endeavor for the morrow. Whenever, therefore, the Alice Freeman Palmer chimes are installed, it would be my wish to have a special cadence rung for our athletes who are in training, perhaps five to ten minutes after the regular chimes at ten o'clock.

Students gather to inspect the first issue of the campus yearbook Cap & Gown, *1895*

*William Rainey Harper presides at
the cornerstone-laying ceremonies for
Stuart Hall (formerly the Law School)
in 1903. President Theodore Roosevelt
is seated in the center of the photo.*

The Professional Programs

In his first *Official Bulletin*, President Harper had projected professional programs in theology, law, medicine, engineering, education, fine arts, and music. He also mentioned an undergraduate College of Practical Arts, which would prepare the student for the "practical aspects of business life." Only the Schools of Divinity, Education, and Law were established during Harper's lifetime, and the School of Business came later, building on Harper's plans.

When the Baptist Union Theological Seminary merged with the University and was transformed into the Divinity School, a denominational seminary preparing men for the ministry became an institution that prepared teachers as well as ministers. Following the example of the graduate curricula in arts and sciences, the professional program of the Divinity School tended to be shaped and defined by scholarly goals. Through the work of Ernest D. Burton, Charles R. Henderson, E. S. Ames, and others, the traditional exegetic and historical dimensions of the theological curriculum were expanded into a critical investigation of the relationships between religious and cultural phenomena.

Charles R. Henderson

The socio-historical method was employed by the Dean of the Divinity School, Shailer Mathews, who had taught "secular" history at Colby during the administration of Albion Small. One of Mathews's first books written at Chicago was the *Social Teaching of Jesus*, which first appeared as a series of articles in the *American Journal of Sociology*. Uniting sociological analysis with biblical exegesis, this study was one of the first to anticipate the concerns of the "social gospel movement" that dominated much Protestant thought during the first decades of the twentieth century. Mathews's influence was recognized by Walter Rauschenbusch, a leading figure in the movement.

The most controversial professor in the Divinity School during its early years was George Burman Foster. In 1906, Foster's book, *The Finality of the Christian Religion*, was published by the University of Chicago Press; it was the first major theological study issued by the Press and it created a furor. The unconventional views of the author were denounced from pulpits and debated in religious journals and the secular press. Irate clergy and anxious parents wrote to the University, demanding to know if the school endorsed such views and if it did not, why it permitted one who espoused such opinions to teach on its faculty. One of the more temperate responses to Foster's book came from President Mullins of Southern Baptist Theological Seminary:

Dr. Foster is evidently a very strong thinker and writer, though, as I tried to show, I think he is inconsistent. I think, however, that the part of wisdom is not to throw stones at him and denounce him, but to answer him. If he cannot be answered, then his positions will stand.

In 1905, three years after William James delivered his famous Gifford lectures on the varieties of religious experience, one of the first courses in the psychology of religion was announced at the University. It was presented by Edward Scribner Ames, minister of the University Church of the Disciples of Christ, who had earned his Ph.D. under John Dewey and James H. Tufts in 1895.

Although graduate instruction in education had started when Dewey organized the Department of Pedagogy in 1894, the School of Education was not organized until seven years later. In 1901, under the aegis of President Harper, three institutions—the Chicago Institute, the South Side Academy, and the Chicago Manual Training School—agreed to join with the Department of Pedagogy to form the School of Education. The merger was made official on July 1, 1901, and at the June 1901 Convocation, ground was broken for Emmons Blaine Hall. Colonel Francis W. Parker of the Chicago Institute became Director of the School of Education, while Dewey remained head Professor of Pedagogy in the Graduate Schools of Arts, Literature, and Science.

A collaboration between the two outstanding educators promised significant achievement. Their approaches were complementary: Dewey was a critical philosopher of education, Parker an intuitive teacher. Dewey once referred to Parker as the "father of the progressive education movement." When Colonel Parker died in 1902, the trustees of the Chicago Institute recommended that Dewey be appointed Director. The man who had established graduate education work at the University became responsible for the professional program.

Some years earlier Dewey had written a memorandum

Haskell Hall Library

George Burman Foster

Students in the Laboratory School
in Blaine Hall

John Dewey

calling for a program that tested educational theory in the reality of the classroom:

The mere profession of principles without their practical exhibition and testing will not engage the respect of the educational profession. Without it, moreover, the theoretical work partakes of the nature of a farce and imposture — it is like professing to give thorough training in a science and then neglecting to provide a laboratory for faculty and students to work in.

In 1896, Dewey established a laboratory school to serve as a workshop for classroom observation and the testing of educational method. Known as the Dewey School, this educational experiment proved so successful that it grew into a series of Laboratory Schools, reaching from kindergarten to the University High School. Although Dewey left the University in 1904, the Laboratory Schools continued to serve as an important center for curricular innovation.

Movement toward creating a professional school of law began in 1894 when the Department of Political Economy introduced a course in "Roman Law and Jurisprudence," taught by a young New York attorney, Ernst Freund, who had done graduate work in Berlin and Heidelberg. When Rockefeller provided funds for the establishment of the Law School in 1902, Freund drafted a proposed curriculum outline for President Harper. In addition to the standard legal courses, the second and third years of the program included subjects that were not part of the traditional legal curriculum but that would, Freund predicted, become of increasing importance to legal studies. These courses covered a range of topics, from psychology and urban sociology to economics and diplomatic history. At Freund's suggestion, Harper sought the advice of the faculty and dean of the Harvard Law School, and Joseph H. Beale consented to take a leave of absence from Harvard to organize and serve as the first Dean of the Chicago Law School.

The University required the bachelor's degree for admission—as few other law schools did at this time. The Harvard curriculum, based on the examination of court cases, did not include the extralegal courses advocated by Freund; this required a compromise between his views and Harvard practice. The first announcement of the course of study provided a three-year program, the first year of which could coincide with the last year of collegiate studies for Chicago undergraduates. Freund's extralegal subjects reappeared as required "prelegal" courses to be taken during the student's undergraduate training.

A collection of law books, valued at $18,000, was purchased with funds provided by Rockefeller, and classes began in October 1902

Floyd Mechem

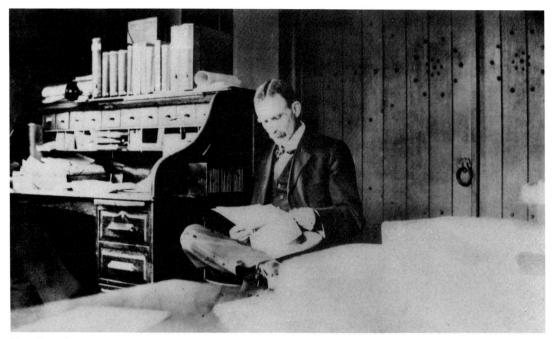

Ernst Freund

in the newly built University Press building. Plans for a permanent
building to be financed by Rockefeller were prepared, and the next
year the ceremony of laying the cornerstone was enhanced by the
presence of President Theodore Roosevelt.

The faculty of the new Law School were predominantly
young men with distinguished careers before them. After Beale
returned to Harvard in 1904, James Parker Hall, an authority on torts
and constitutional law, succeeded him as Dean. Floyd Mechem, who
would later be well known for his writings in the field of sales and
agency, came to Chicago from the University of Michigan; like Hall
and Freund, he remained at the University for his entire career. Julian
Mack, on the other hand, having come to the Law School with a
reputation as one of the city's most gifted lawyers, subsequently left
the teaching profession and became an outstanding federal judge.
A blend of the practical and the academic was seen in the career of
Freund. In addition to teaching such courses as "Principles of Legislation," Freund utilized his knowledge of the law to draft or revise social
legislation in cooperation with leading social agencies.

The Department of Political Economy not only sponsored
the University's initial work in jurisprudence; it also fathered the
School of Business. In 1894, Laughlin presented a proposal to the
University Senate to organize a professional program in business
administration. After four years of debate, the College of Commerce

and Politics was established. As the name implied, the new venture was not a professional school but an undergraduate program. Since the College did not yet have its own faculty, its courses were drawn from the existing offerings of the Departments of Sociology, Political Science, History, and Political Economy. Two years later the name was changed to the College of Commerce and Administration, and in 1902 the first dean of the College, Henry Rand Hatfield, was appointed.

It was Laughlin who prepared the text of the first bulletin of the College of Commerce and Politics in 1898. As his draft of the bulletin made plain, Laughlin believed that business, like divinity, medicine, or law, was a profession that required specialized preparation. At that time only the Wharton School in Philadelphia offered business education within a university context. Laughlin saw the work in commerce and politics as

another step in the movement by which University education is being adapted to the life of the community. The rise of economic, social and political problems, together with the phenomenal industrial development of our country, demands that training should be given fit to deal with them.

He proposed a curriculum combining liberal arts with specialized studies in railway management, banking, insurance, trade and industry, politics, and journalism. These ambitious plans required years for even partial realization. After 1916, the School of Commerce and Administration emerged as a separate administrative unit and as a graduate professional school.

James Parker Hall

J. Laurence Laughlin

The School and Society, *by John Dewey, published by the University Press in 1899*

University Extension and the University Press

The University's ambitious program for adult education brought together two significant British and American educational developments of the late nineteenth century. Lectures on a variety of edifying topics had become enormously popular in both countries. They were frequently delivered to the general public outside the boundaries of academic institutions, often in smaller towns. Subsequently, Cambridge University in England took the lead in sponsoring such extramural lectures. In this country, summer lecture courses given at Chautauqua, New York, under the auspices of the Methodist church, drew thousands of visitors to the lakeside resort in the southwestern corner of the state. Correspondence courses offering instruction in a variety of subjects through the mails were likewise popular.

Through the success of his own correspondence courses in Hebrew and his participation in the Chautauqua program, Harper had become convinced that Chicago should make a strong effort to disseminate knowledge beyond the regular classroom. The University Extension Division was organized to make learning available to the wider community. Although Harper's plan underwent considerable modification, it was the basis for the University's commitment to adult education.

Initially, the work of the Extension Division took three forms: lectures delivered off campus, class study in downtown Chicago, and correspondence courses. During the first years the emphasis was on lecture study. Syllabuses were prepared in advance and many of the faculty participated in extension work; sometimes a single topic brought together members of the faculty from quite different disciplines in a single series of lectures. In 1897, for example, a lecture series titled "Life After Death" was prepared by a group so diverse as to include Albion Small, James H. Breasted, Paul Shorey, Emil Hirsch, Thomas C. Chamberlin, and President Harper.

The most prominent extension lecturer was Richard Green

Richard Green Moulton

Galley trays in racks and galley proofs, fourth floor, Press building, 1913

Job bindery, third floor, Press building, 1913

Moulton, who had lectured for the Cambridge University program for sixteen years before he was persuaded to come to Chicago. Moulton accepted the Chicago invitation because he was impressed by Harper's knowledge of the British extension system and by the strength of the University's commitment to extension work. When Nathaniel Butler was preparing to represent the University at a conference in England, Moulton wrote to Harper:

> Not only do I want the position of Chicago emphasized—for I claim a leadership for this University on the ground of its being the first to make Extension an organic part of a first-rank university—but I am equally anxious for the director of our division to have the fullest experience of English work.

As the primary mode of adult education, lecture study eventually proved ineffective. It was difficult to adopt an examination system easily related to the popular lecture format, and gradually emphasis shifted to the courses given by the Class Study Department. In 1898, the University established a college for public school teachers who had little or no training beyond a high school education. It soon became apparent that the College for Teachers and the Class Study Department duplicated programs for the same constituency. Consequently, they were merged into University College, as the University's extension program was to be known for many years. Harper's continuing interest in adult education revealed itself in a letter to Dean Mathews of the Divinity School, proposing two "good, strong" courses in Bible study: "Is not something of this kind really important? Is it not worth trying?"

If the University's extension program sought to provide learning opportunities for the general public, the University Press undertook to disseminate knowledge to a largely scholarly audience. The Press of course served the immediate University community by publishing departmental announcements, syllabuses, calendars, and other official documents, while a wider public composed of alumni, Trustees, and friends of the University were kept informed of University plans, achievements, and noteworthy events through publications like the *Weekly University Record*.

Harper's plan called for the Press to be a major publisher of scholarly books, monographs, and journals. It was some time before this hope could be fully realized, for the early years of the Press were not easy. During the first two years of its existence, the Press was a legal entity separate from the University, operated by the Boston publishing house of D. C. Heath in conjunction with the Chicago printer R. R. Donnelley. The arrangement proved unworkable, however, and by mutual and amicable agreement the University secured

D. C. Heath

the sole ownership of its publishing division in 1894. Some years later, D. C. Heath came across a statement he had prepared in 1892 setting forth the aims of the Press. It read in part:

This is the age of books (Carlyle's University) and preeminently the age of discovery. Therefore it is the age of a progressive and rapid revelation of new truth and of the periodical publication of the truth for the benefit of others working or studying along kindred lines. President Harper not only believes that the best teacher is one who, like Agassiz, is an investigator *with* his pupil for the establishment of an old truth and the discovery of the new, but the one who inspires his students to independent and never ceasing investigation. He also believes that the worthy results of all this work should be published first for the sake of its reflex influence on students and teachers, and second that it may aid others who are working in the same line.

Like many other parts of the University during the formative era, the Press was handicapped by inadequate facilities. One member of the printing department staff wrote plaintively to President Harper requesting more equipment, better sanitary facilities, and a promotion. By 1900, the situation had improved with the appointment of the energetic Newman Miller as Director, and two years later the new Press building, the first substantial work erected on campus by the architectural firm of Shepley, Rutan, and Coolidge, provided much needed space. The relief was not total, however, as the building also housed the library, bookstore, and various administrative offices.

In 1902, the Press began a venture which proved to be one of the most ambitious and important in American academic publishing history. As part of the celebration of the University's tenth anniversary, it undertook a project that ultimately resulted in a set of twenty-eight volumes known as the "Decennial Publications." This series comprised reports of the President and administrative officers detailing the achievements of the first decade, a collection of scholarly articles representing research in each of the departments, and individual studies reporting substantial original research by such professors as A. A. Michelson, John Dewey, Sophonisba Breckinridge, W. G. Hale, Thomas C. Chamberlin, and Jacques Loeb. In order to prepare such a large quantity of material for publication, the Press organized a copy-editing and proofreading section to prepare guidelines for standard usage. The result of their work was *A Manual of Style*, published in 1906, which has since become a widely accepted standard for editorial practice in the United States.

Press building from southeast

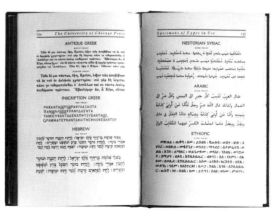

Type specimens from the first edition of
A Manual of Style, *1906*

The Library

The original plans for the University had called for a majestic library building on Ellis Avenue at 58th Street. Ten years after that plan was adopted, the site remained vacant, and President Harper declared that the erection of such a facility was imperative. Despite the lack of a central library building, the University nonetheless possessed a great library when it opened. The remarkable book holdings of the Baptist Union Theological Seminary and the Berlin Collection (chosen by Harper himself when the entire stock of a well-known German bookdealer went on sale) were unparalleled resources for teaching and research in the Middle West.

Harper had hoped that Melvil Dewey, then at Columbia, would accept the directorship of the University Library. Dewey had reacted with much enthusiasm to the Chicago plans and was tantalizingly responsive to the courtship. In the end, however, he remained at Columbia, and the directorship of the library stayed vacant until 1910, when Ernest DeWitt Burton added that post to his teaching positions. General supervision of the book collections rested, from 1891 until 1910, with Zella Allen Dixson, who had been the librarian of the Baptist Union Theological Seminary. Dixson had studied with Dewey, who described her as "an earnest, enthusiastic and successful apostle of the new library movement."

The general library of the University initially occupied a room in Cobb Hall. On January 3, 1893, it moved into a temporary building on 57th Street, sharing this space with the University Press and the gymnasium. Departmental libraries were established as lecture halls and laboratories were built; this lessened the overcrowding of the general library and placed books and classrooms in greater proximity.

By 1901, the absence of an adequate central library building and of a head librarian had produced an inefficient and inconvenient library system spread across campus. It was necessary to purchase duplicate copies of books that did not fall into obvious subject classi-

Zella Allen Dixson

fications or that were needed for both undergraduate and graduate
courses, and some of the departmental libraries took a distinctly
proprietary attitude toward books in their possession. A committee
was formed to study the situation, and the faculty was asked to state its
preference between a centralized and a departmental library system.
Charles O. Whitman spoke for the overwhelming majority of the
natural scientists when he reported to the committee the view of the
Department of Zoology:

> In our opinion the departmental library must always be maintained as near ideal
> completeness as possible, regardless of the cost involved in duplication of many
> books of reference. The Departmental Library should under no circumstances be
> weakened for the sake of a General Library.

Those in the humanities and the professional schools looked
with more favor on a central library. Representing the Departments of
Philosophy and Education, John Dewey presented a carefully hedged
preference:

> I am in favor of a central library provided there is provision for a seminar and
> departmental library of good size; also upon condition that the administrative
> methods are such as to retain to the department much of their present control of
> departmental libraries on the intellectual side—that is as to number, character of
> books, etc.; also on condition that this does not preclude still further specialized
> departmental libraries in connection with laboratories or even with particular
> courses where it is desirable to have books close at hand. Unless there is provision
> of this sort, I am in favor of retaining our present system.

The result of this preliminary investigation was the creation
of the Commission on Library Building and Policy chaired by Burton.
In 1902, the commission made its recommendations: it proposed that
a library building be erected on the south side of the Quadrangles,
rather than at the Ellis and 58th Street site, in close conjunction with
the departmental libraries in the already existing buildings and in
anticipation of the new buildings proposed for Classics, Modern
Languages, History and Social Sciences, Divinity, Law, and Philosophy. It further recommended greater cooperation among the libraries
of the science group on the north side of the campus. It was the
implementation of this plan that President Harper urged in his report
on the University's tenth anniversary.

On January 10, 1906, President Harper died at the age
of forty-nine years. He had become President of the University of
Chicago at the age of thirty-four and for many years had carried out
strenuous and diverse tasks with extraordinary vigor. Early in 1905,
he learned that he was suffering from cancer, and surgery confirmed
that the illness was terminal.

Ernest DeWitt Burton

A departmental library in Cobb Hall, ca. 1890s

*The library, gymnasium, and University
Press building, from the southeast*

Winter on the Quadrangles, ca. 1911
(Hull Gate in foreground)

After his death it seemed appropriate to erect this long-desired central library building as his memorial. Martin Ryerson and Charles Hutchinson presented the idea to the Trustees, and, as the former wrote to Andrew MacLeish, "They strongly favor the erection of a library building as a memorial to President Harper. We all agreed that the earliest possible action is desirable." Rockefeller pledged $800,000 toward the cost of the building if an additional $200,000 could be raised. This was readily accomplished, and Shepley, Rutan, and Coolidge were commissioned to prepare plans.

The cornerstone for the William Rainey Harper Memorial Library was laid on June 14, 1910, by Mrs. Harper. Construction proceeded according to schedule; then, on May 29, 1911, workmen on the roof of the west tower were moving a derrick from a corner to the center of the roof when it began to give way. Attempts were made to place support braces under the roof and some of the lower floors. When the alarm sounded, the workmen on the various floors ran into the central portion of the building just as the tower roof collapsed onto the sixth floor. The sixth floor gave way, carrying all the lower floors into the basement; a section of the outer south wall of the tower also collapsed. The workmen were able to jump free in time, but the construction superintendent, who was climbing between the third and fourth floors, did not hear the alarm. He took refuge under the stairs, which held in place, and he was bruised but not seriously hurt.

With everyone shaken but grateful, work was soon resumed and the building—with a new west tower—was completed the following year. On June 11, 1912, the library was dedicated. Tributes to President Harper were delivered, and the architect, Charles A. Coolidge, spoke on the educational significance of university architecture. Twenty years after the founding of the University, the central library projected in Harper's original plan was a reality.

Collapse of the west tower of Harper Library

The Masque, "The Gift" — Edith
Foster Flint as Alma Mater

The Quarter Centennial and
Its Aftermath

The era immediately following President Harper's death seemed, in retrospect, less exciting and innovative than the founding years. Set firmly on course, the institution had realized many of its initial goals. Under President Harry Pratt Judson (1907–23), ferment gave way to sober analysis of the University's needs and to consolidation of its resources. Features of the original educational design that proved to be of marginal importance — the Class Study Department of the University Extension Division and the academy at Morgan Park — were eliminated. In 1909, for the first time, the University ended its fiscal year with a balanced budget. Rockefeller's pleasure at the financial stability was readily apparent: from 1906 until his final gift in 1910, he more than equaled his previous benefactions and brought his total gifts to the University to nearly $35 million.

In an age of great private fortunes, John D. Rockefeller was remarkable in taking philanthropy as seriously as he took business. He considered the administration of his fortune to have a moral dimension, and he viewed his philanthropic endeavors as consequential investments. He sought to direct his wealth to enterprises of demonstrable value that, in the long term, would possess a significance beyond the immediate outlay.

Besieged by requests for donations, Rockefeller established the General Education Board, later to become the Rockefeller Foundation, as the channel through which he continued his philanthropies. Frederick Gates became Rockefeller's chief adviser through whom all financial appeals were to be made. In this way Rockefeller separated his personal relationship with Harper and other members of the University community from his financial commitment. Beyond his concern for fiscal responsibility, Rockefeller declined to exercise influence on academic life.

In 1910, Rockefeller announced a final gift to the University of $10 million, declaring:

Masque of Youth mural in Ida Noyes Hall third-floor theater

Dean Talbot speaking at the cornerstone laying of Ida Noyes Hall.
La Verne Noyes (in top hat) is seated on the left.

It is far better that the University be supported and enlarged by the gifts of many than of a single donor. This I have recognized from the beginning and, accordingly have sought to assist you in enlisting the interest and securing the contributions of many others, at times by making my own gifts conditional on the gifts of others, and at times by aiding you by means of unconditional gifts to make the University as widely useful, worthy and attractive as possible . . . In the multitude of students so quickly gathered, in the high character of the instruction, in the variety and extent of original research, in the valuable contributions to human knowledge, in the uplifting influence of the University as a whole upon education throughout the West, my highest hopes have been far exceeded. . . . This gift completes the task which I have set before myself.

In the year of the final gift, a committee was appointed to prepare for the twenty-fifth anniversary of the founding, to be celebrated in 1916. Plans were made for a week of commemorative activities both serious and informal. The fiftieth anniversary of the Divinity School was also to be celebrated. Returning alumni flocked to the celebration, each class marching onto Stagg Field. Hijinks followed: a circus, a chariot race, and a series of skits including "Harper Library; or, Asleep in the Stacks." The major athletic event of the day was a baseball game which matched the University's team with the players from Waseda University in Japan—an international series which had begun in 1910.

In a commemorative address President Judson offered some notable statistics about the University: since its founding, 57,000 students had matriculated, the original three buildings on ten acres had become forty buildings on one hundred acres, and $37.5 million had been given to the University, with an additional $500,000 pledged.

The high point of the Quarter Centennial was the dedication of Ida Noyes Hall. In May 1913, the Chicago businessman La Verne Noyes offered the University $300,000 for a women's building as a memorial to his wife. For many years funds for such a building had been sought, particularly after Reynolds Clubhouse had been built for the men in 1903. The architects, Shepley, Rutan, and Coolidge, designed a building so remarkable in its blending of the formal and the gracious that Mr. Noyes contributed an additional $200,000 in order to fulfill the original conception. Ida Noyes Hall was dedicated on June 5, 1916, with pomp and ceremony. Two hundred and fifty faculty and students presented a masque, "The Gift," before an audience of three thousand. The masque portrayed, in allegorical dance and mime, the stages of education. Some years later the walls of the theater in Ida Noyes Hall were decorated with a mural depicting the masque.

The Quarter Centennial observance also occasioned the publication of the first history of the University. Thomas W. Goodspeed, who was intimately involved in all stages of that history, devoted three years to the project. His *History of the University of Chicago, The First Quarter Century* is not only a personal account, but a heavily documented history in the words of the principal participants. Goodspeed was indebted to Frederick Gates, who had preserved much of the original correspondence surrounding the founding.

The celebration marked the University's rise and the fulfillment of the aspirations of its founders. Goodspeed's retelling of the achievements of the early years and the activities during the week of celebration created within the University community a new self-awareness. The year 1916 signaled the end of an era in the life of the institution, and for many the final lines of the convocation ode rang true in capturing the relationship among the parts of the University:

Harper to Ryerson speaks, and all your towers
Mysteriously answer to the spell:
"All is well,
All is well!
We guard the eternal mind!
The heart of man retains its ancient powers,
And with the eternal spirit all is well!"

Ida Noyes

In 1924 the Prince of Wales visited
the University. Here he shares a joke
with a Salvation Army worker, Frank
Billings, and President Burton.

Harry Pratt Judson and John D. Rockefeller, Jr.

Renewal, not complacency, characterized the University during the years following the Quarter Centennial. The presidency of Ernest DeWitt Burton, although brief (1923–25), was among the most distinguished in the institution's history. Burton's administration reaffirmed the commitment to educational innovation and laid the foundation for many significant achievements that materialized under his successors. Chosen Acting President at the age of sixty-seven in 1923, Burton so impressed the Trustees with his energy that they appointed him to the presidency the same year. At the time of his sudden death two years later, the University had embarked on a plan for its future development conducted with an enthusiasm not seen since the Harper era. President Burton felt that Rockefeller's final gift of $10 million challenged the University to accept full responsibility for its future.

Accordingly, the University began its first major development campaign in 1924, in recognition that "the great task of the University in the next fifteen years is to bring all its work, in all departments and schools, up to an even higher level than has yet been attained." The sum of $17.5 million was sought to complete the architectural program for the campus and to provide for research and teaching needs. The School of Medicine was founded and construction of the hospitals and clinics begun. Buildings were provided for the social sciences, modern languages, and mathematics, along with much-needed additional facilities for chemistry and education. Work began on the University Chapel, and plans were developed for an administration building and expanded library facilities. Graduate studies and the needs of the undergraduates were reevaluated. There was a widespread feeling on the Quadrangles that the University was entering a new epoch.

Alumni reunion parade, 1923

Dr. Frank Billings (center left),
a nephew of Albert Merritt Billings,
and James H. Tufts, vice president
of the University (center right)
among dignitaries at the dedication
of the Albert Merritt Billings
Hospital, 1927

A School of Medicine

A medical school had been part of Harper's plan, but during the University's first thirty years medical education was carried out in cooperation with Rush Medical College, which had trained Chicago physicians since 1837. An affiliation between Rush and the University took place in 1898, and by 1901 the preclinical courses were taught in the Ogden (Graduate) School of Science, while the clinical program was conducted at Rush Medical College's west side buildings.

A major difference of opinion developed, however, about the desirability of formal union. Although President Harper came to favor such a merger, others felt that the wiser course lay in establishing a new medical school devoted exclusively to research. The matter remained unresolved at the time of Harper's death.

Reassessment of the University's medical program began in 1916 with a study conducted by the General Education Board, which noted Chicago's unique opportunity for creating a complete integration of professional training. By organizing a medical school and clinics on campus, instruction and patient care could be carried on jointly with medical research in the science laboratories. No other university in the country had been able to develop such an integrated approach. The hospitals of Johns Hopkins and Harvard, for example, were at some distance from their central campuses. The cost of initiating the plan was estimated to be $5.3 million; the General Education Board pledged $2 million if the remainder could be obtained. Within a relatively short time the University had raised this amount. However, implementation was delayed by the intervention of World War I and by postwar inflation.

In 1923, the medical program received "a new impetus" under President Burton, according to Dr. Frank Billings. The following year the School of Medicine was established, Rush Medical College was united with the University as its postgraduate School of Medicine, and the University Hospitals were established. Ground

Frank R. Lillie

was broken for the Albert Merritt Billings Hospital on May 7, 1925. With the opening of that facility in 1927, an integrated medical program was under way.

The first departments organized under the School of Medicine—Medicine and Surgery—joined such long-established departments as Anatomy, Physiology, Hygiene and Bacteriology, and Zoology, which had been devoted to research since the earliest years of the University. The integrated medical program, while ground-breaking, was heir to a strong scientific legacy, and many of the men who had made significant contributions in fields related to medicine now participated directly in medical teaching and research.

Frank R. Lillie had been appointed Assistant Professor of Embryology in 1900, six years after he received his Ph.D. at the University under the direction of Charles O. Whitman. Lillie was equally at home in teaching, research, and administration. He succeeded Whitman as Zoology Department Chairman and as Director of the Marine Biological Laboratory at Woods Hole, Massachusetts. After the reorganization of the University in 1930, he became the first Dean of the Biological Sciences Division. Throughout his life, Lillie worked primarily in the area of experimental embryology. His book *The Development of the Chick* (1908) is a classic text in this field, and his discovery of the importance of embryonic sex hormones in sexual differentiation has been termed his greatest scientific contribution. During his tenure as Chairman and Dean, Lillie gave high importance to the teaching of both graduates and undergraduates (in contrast to the stance of his brilliant but quixotic predecessor, Whitman, who refused to teach undergraduates and whose graduate students often had to ferret him out of his home).

The first and for some years the most successful survey course in the College, "The Nature of the World and of Man," was inaugurated by Lillie and his colleagues, principally H. H. Newman. Lillie's graduate course in embryology was a required course in the medical school. In 1924, Lillie and his wife gave $60,000 "toward the development of the University with the proviso that it be used to erect a building for Experimental Zoology." In 1926, the Charles Otis Whitman Laboratory for Experimental Zoology was dedicated.

Microbiology developed at the School of Medicine under the aegis of Edwin O. Jordan. Work in bacteriology had begun at the University in 1895, and a separate Department of Bacteriology was set up under Jordan's direction in 1913. Jordan was a gifted teacher and many of the leading microbiologists of the next generation were his students. He helped organize the Society of American Bacteriologists

Edwin O. Jordan

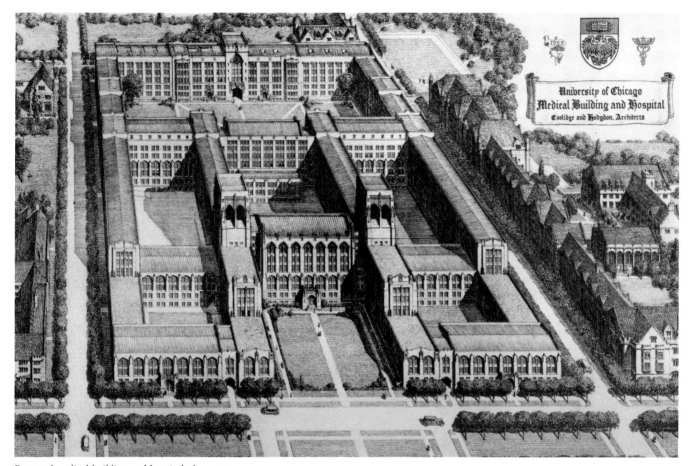

Proposed medical building and hospital plan, 1925

and the American Epidemiological Society, and for many years he edited the *Journal of Infectious Diseases* and the *Journal of Preventive Medicine*. Since he was less interested in the cure of diseases than in their prevention, his research work focused on problems of public health. Health agencies, from the local to the international level, often sought his advice, and he was widely known for his work on food poisoning and influenza. He was the first to investigate in great detail the self–purification of streams. As his lectures on the history of bacteriology indicate, Jordan approached the discipline historically:

The consideration of a few phases in the developmental history of bacteriology may enable us to estimate the present tendencies and importance of the science more justly than could a simple review of existing facts and theories—just as the embryology of an organism in connection with its adult structure enables us to form a better conception of its nature and relations than a study of the adult structure alone.

In 1922, the noted Russian histologist, Alexander A. Maximow, joined the Department of Anatomy. Although he had been offered the post in 1918, the turmoil of the Russian Revolution

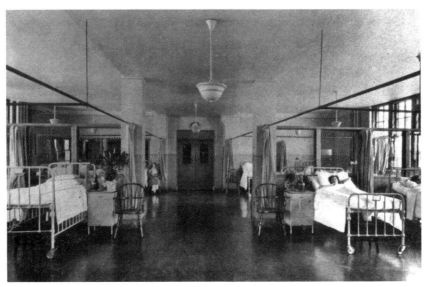

Typical sixteen-bed pavilion in Billings Hospital, 1931

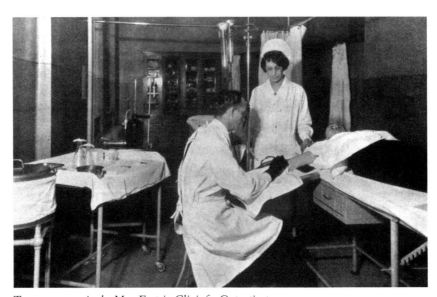

Treatment room in the Max Epstein Clinic for Outpatients, 1931

prevented him from leaving his country. Aided by University funds, Maximow escaped across the Gulf of Finland. An internationally recognized authority on the nature of blood and connective tissue, Maximow continued at Chicago his research on living tissue. In 1924, he contributed toward the cure of tuberculosis when he reproduced the disease in isolated lung tissue of rabbits. The results of this experiment were published in the *Journal of Infectious Diseases,* along with drawings of exceptional quality that Maximow customarily produced to illustrate his texts. Just before leaving Russia, Maximow published his two-volume *Principles of Histology,* and he was preparing an English text at the time of his death in 1928. Drawing on sections of the older work, his colleague, William Bloom, edited and completed Maximow's book, and *A Textbook of Histology* was first published in 1930.

Alexander A. Maximow

The University of Chicago settlement

The City as Social Laboratory

The early decades of the University coincided with a period when the city of Chicago was widely regarded throughout the world, by curious observer and social analyst alike, as the prime example of the evolving industrial and commercial metropolis that seemed destined to characterize modern times. Novelists, poets, journalists—Theodore Dreiser, Robert Herrick, Upton Sinclair, Carl Sandburg, Lincoln Steffens—turned to Chicago for urban themes. When the English journalist W. T. Stead wrote an account of the social problems developing in this new kind of city, he gave his work the provocative title *If Christ Came to Chicago*. The Columbian Exposition had of course served to place Chicago and its situation under a particularly bright spotlight.

The first generation of University social scientists believed that effecting social change was as important as studying it. Members of the faculty were instrumental in founding a settlement house in 1894. The University of Chicago settlement, located in the neighborhood of the Union Stockyards, served as a social center for the disadvantaged, a practicum for social workers (initially known as "social engineers"), and a training ground for sociologists.

The continued growth of urban centers and of social problems challenged activists and scholars to discover more comprehensive ways of administering social welfare. A new profession in social work emerged through the efforts of clergymen such as Graham Taylor and educators such as Sophonisba Breckinridge and Grace and Edith Abbott. Their efforts paralleled the work being done in academic sociology and drew heavily upon it.

In 1903, a Social Science Center for Practical Training in Philanthropic and Social Work was organized as part of the University extension program. Under the direction of Graham Taylor, the center sponsored lectures by University faculty and leading settlement workers, including Jane Addams and Julia Lathrop. The success of the program led to its reorganization as the Institute of Social Science and

Edith Abbott

75

Arts; the institute drew more heavily upon the resources of the University, offering courses through the Departments of Sociology, Education, Political Science, and Psychology. During its first year after reorganization, Taylor and John Cummings gave a course in juvenile delinquency, Charles Henderson taught courses in criminology, and John B. Watson offered introductory and advanced psychology. A field-work program was initiated and a Laboratory for Statistical Research Work established. In 1906, the official relationship between the institute and the University was terminated; a grant from the Russell Sage Foundation allowed the institute to create an independent program as the Chicago Institute of Social Science, and later, the Chicago School of Civics and Philanthropy. In fact, the School of Civics and Philanthropy and the University retained close ties; Charles Henderson, Sophonisba Breckinridge, Ernst Freund, and George H. Mead taught on both faculties, and many University professors, notably Albion Small and W. I. Thomas, among the founders of modern urban sociology, lectured at the school.

In 1908, Edith Abbott joined the faculty of the School of Civics and Philanthropy as Associate Director of Research. She had received her Ph.D. from the University in political economy in 1905. Five years later, when her book *Women in Industry: A Study in American Economic History* was published, J. Laurence Laughlin wrote:

It is an epoch-making and remarkably successful piece of work. It is the first thing of its kind in a new field; and no one is ever likely to do anything which would make it obsolete. I am especially proud of the book because its author was once a worker in my Seminar; but the quality of the book is primarily due to the individual abilities and sympathetic outlook of the author.

In 1913, Abbott joined the University faculty as Lecturer in the Department of Sociology in Methods of Social Investigation, at the same time retaining her connection with Civics and Philanthropy.

Shortly thereafter, a plan for affiliating the School of Civics and Philanthropy with the University was proposed, but action was delayed by the war. In 1920, the school, which had begun its professional program in conjunction with the University, joined with the Philanthropic Science Division of the School of Commerce and Administration to form the School of Social Service Administration. Five years after the merger, President Mason sent a copy of a report reviewing the initial achievements of the school to the political scientist Charles Merriam:

I wonder if we thoroughly appreciate what is building here in the social sciences and co-ordinate professional schools. Just as one authority on medical education has pointed out that the University of Chicago has the best opportunity of service

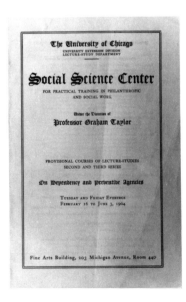

Ernest W. Burgess

in this field of any institution in the country, because of the combination here of high grade departments in the pre-clinical sciences, adequate professional schools and clinics for practical work, so we are developing toward a similar three-fold equipment in the social service field. We have sound and growing departments in the basic social sciences, we have a professional school of great promise and clinical opportunities for practical work of service in many contacts with the Chicago community.

The task of directing the social work program rested primarily on Abbott, who was named Dean in 1924. Throughout her career, she continued her work on women in industry, strengthened the academic requirements for professional social work, and stressed the importance of active inquiry on such topics as population and housing conditions in Chicago, social work methodology, social legislation, child welfare, women in industry, and crime. In 1934, when Grace Abbott resigned from the United States Children's Bureau to join her sister on the Chicago faculty, she brought to the school her extensive experience with problems of child labor and health.

During this same period, in the Department of Sociology, the second generation of Chicago scholars combined a lively interest in the development of theory with a scrupulous inspection of the urban scene. Thus, Robert E. Park's *Introduction to the Science of Sociology* was published in 1921. Then, four years later, *The City,* edited by Park and Ernest W. Burgess with a bibliography by Louis Wirth, was published. So extensive was the research in urban sociology done under Park, Burgess, and Wirth that "Chicago Sociology" during this period became synonymous with urban studies.

Park was the oldest of the three collaborators. During a career as a newspaper reporter, he gradually turned from journalism to a fascination with the problems of the city, undertaking graduate study at Harvard. Before receiving his Ph.D. in 1903, Park studied in Germany and became conversant with European sociological theory. After graduation he accepted a post as secretary to Booker T. Washington at Tuskegee Institute and studied race relations in the South. In 1913, he joined the Chicago faculty.

Burgess had been trained by the first generation of Chicago sociologists, receiving his Ph.D. in 1913 and joining the faculty in 1919. Taking over many of the courses previously taught by Charles Henderson, Burgess developed such concerns as the sociology of the family, social pathology, and criminology into full-fledged branches of social science.

Park and Burgess continued and expanded the older tradition of active investigation into urban problems. Research projects were carried on in conjunction with allied work in political science, economics, psychology, and history. Students were encouraged to pursue their inquiries through personal involvement coupled with strict empiricism. The stress on objectivity did not preclude a concern with general principles or presuppositions. Park, especially, stimulated his students to consider theoretical questions. His introduction to a course on "Methods of Social Research," given during the Spring Quarter of 1927, stated:

Robert E. Park

We should in this course browse around and take time to look at ourselves from the outside. We should take time to get acquainted with the literature on the margin of our field. We should look at our field from a general philosophical viewpoint. I have been impressed with the fact that while people may be quite keen and good in their own fields, when they come to attack a problem which is slightly outside their own field but even closely related, they are at a great loss. It seems to me to be due to the fact that they do not have any fundamental conception of what science is.

Students of Park and Burgess conducted energetic explorations of Chicago, examining diverse areas of urban ecology and behavior. Among these studies were Nels Anderson's *The Hobo*, E. R. Mowrer's *Family Disorganization*, E. Franklin Frazer's *The Negro Family in Chicago*, John Landesco's *Organized Crime in Chicago*, and Wirth's *The Ghetto*. One of the best-known of Burgess's own concepts was his zonal hypothesis, which projected a pattern of more or less homogeneous areas to be found in large, industrial, developing cities. Burgess offered the zonal theory as a tool for understanding urban behavior, including variations in patterns of family life.

The junior member of this group of urban analysts was Wirth, who began his sociological studies as an undergraduate. During the summer between his junior and senior years, for example, he prepared a paper on prostitution at Chicago's public beaches for Burgess's course on Social Pathology, commenting wryly:

In these earnest days of war it is rather difficult to contemplate on such a topic; but one can find consolation in the fact that on the beach as on the battlefield we can see human nature and particularly the most primitive impulses working equally well. Both offer equal opportunities for study to the student and the role of the former is in the long run as productive of results as the latter although at the present time we all are more anxious to discover the method of controlling Moloch than to enslave the evil forces of Venus . . . . We shall limit ourself to that part of the life at the beach which centers around the sex impulse, bringing in other aspects of the subject only insofar as they have a direct bearing upon our center of interest.

Observing the fascinated gaze that Chicago intellectuals bent upon their city, Richard Wright, the novelist, noted in his introduction to *Black Metropolis* (1945) that "Chicago is the *known* city; perhaps more is known about it, how it is run, how it kills, how it loves, steals, helps, gives, cheats, and crushes than any other city in the world." Wright gives credit for this knowledge to such local writers as Carl Sandburg, Nelson Algren, and James Farrell, but he reserved his greatest admiration for the sociologists at the University of Chicago, the Parks, Frazers, and Wirths, who "relied upon the city for their basic truth of America's social life" and who were "not afraid to urge their students to trust their feelings for a situation or an event."

The Reform of Undergraduate Education

Throughout the 1920s, the original tension between Rockefeller's preference for a college at Chicago and Harper's development of a full-fledged university remained very much alive. Harper's emphasis on graduate work and the subsequent achievements of the University in research caused many to question the place of the undergraduate Colleges. When Burton assumed the presidency, the original plan for the Junior College as an instrument of general education remained undeveloped. In 1923, with more than 3,500 students enrolled in the Colleges of Arts, Literature, and Science, much of the teaching, particularly in the Junior College, was done by graduate students. Freshmen were encouraged to determine their educational goals as early as possible and plan their course work accordingly. There was some faculty sentiment to abolish the undergraduate program altogether.

President Burton regarded eminence in research as an asset, rather than an obstacle, in organizing an undergraduate program of first quality. What students needed to fit them for later life, he believed, was not the "mere passing on of more or less standardized knowledge," but rather "initiative; the capacity to think for themselves; to do the things they must do, with the greatest efficiency." These intellectual habits were fostered in the atmosphere of the great graduate schools, "where freedom of the mind is encouraged, and where fine libraries and good laboratories furnish the best means for independent study."

President Burton took a first step toward what Harold Swift called his "dream of the colleges" by appointing a Commission on the Future of the Colleges in September 1923. Headed by Ernest H. Wilkins, recently appointed Dean of the Colleges, the commission emphasized the centrality of "general education," defined as:

the attainment of independence in thinking in which civilized societies of the past and of the present have done and are doing their thinking; . . . independence in

Ernest H. Wilkins

On opposite page: Participants in the Two-Year High School Entrants' Program, 1940s appreciation of the fine arts, and the absorption of the fine arts into the individual's life; . . . independence in moral living.

To achieve these ambitious goals, the report recommended that the undergraduate curriculum be organized under an administrative unit known simply as "The College." The length of time in the College program was to be flexible; an able student could be granted the bachelor's degree after two years of study. Recognizing that high school standards varied greatly, the report recommended that the level of admission to the College be based on an individual analysis of the student's previous achievements. It was further suggested that a closer relationship between the University High School and the College would enable gifted students to gain early admission to the collegiate course of study.

Other recommendations were that the size of the College should be limited to 1,500; that the College faculty be composed of individuals who were primarily teachers, not researchers; and that the College be established as a separate physical entity on the south side of the Midway—although graduates and undergraduates would have equal access to both programs and facilities. Finally, the establishment of the College was seen as part of a general reorganization of the graduate work of the University.

During the brief administration (1925–28) of Max Mason, who succeeded President Burton, there were further refinements in the new College plan. Concluding that the physical separation of undergraduates from the main Quadrangles was not feasible, the planning group set aside proposals for buildings and concentrated on curriculum. The earlier recommendation that the bachelor's degree be granted on the basis of demonstrated competence was now given substance: the student would qualify for the degree by passing a number of comprehensive examinations which could be taken at any time. There would be a minimum one-year residence requirement, and the credit system would be a thing of the past.

Thus, by 1929, when Robert Maynard Hutchins began his tenure as President (1929–51), a constellation of proposals for the reform of collegiate education had already taken shape at Chicago. While Hutchins was still at Yale, Chauncey Boucher, who had succeeded Wilkins as Dean of the College, sent the new President a report of the status of these ideas. Hutchins replied that he had read the report with interest. Once Hutchins was in office, this interest was promptly manifested by strong support for the implementation of many of these proposals, as Dean Boucher and his staff worked on a revised College curriculum known as the "New Plan."

Max Mason

F. Champion Ward

       Central to this curriculum was a series of year-long inter-disciplinary courses devoted to the social sciences, the humanities, and the natural sciences. Initially, however, the bachelor's degree was not conferred after completion of the College program, but only after additional divisional requirements had been met. As early as 1933, Hutchins recommended that the last two years of the University High School and the first two years of undergraduate work be linked, and that the College be empowered to award the bachelor's degree. This design for a four-year College program concerned exclusively with general education was adopted formally in 1942, and became the institutional framework for what was known familiarly as the "Hutchins College."

       Under the leadership of Deans Clarence Faust and F. Champion Ward, the College recruited a separate teaching faculty (although some members continued to hold joint appointments in one of the graduate divisions). Graduation requirements were set in terms of fourteen comprehensive examinations embracing the major scholarly disciplines and skills. Individual professors did not directly grade their students' work; evaluation was made at the end of the year through examination papers read without knowledge of the student's identity. Placement examinations determined how many general-education requirements were to be met; the full fourteen-course roster demanded three and a half years of study, with half a year left over for elective courses. Quadrangles legend had it that the only College entrant

On following pages: Eight hundred students taking placement tests at the Field House, September 24–25, 1945

passing all fourteen requirements by placement test was a young man who had already completed a program of general studies at a *liceo* in Milan, Italy.

All the general-education courses were organized and taught by faculty members drawn from a range of fields. The College made relatively little use of large-audience lectures. Most instruction took place in discussion groups, and since many students were in the same courses and reading the same books, discussions tended to spill over from the classrooms into the residence halls and off-campus hangouts. The liveliness of these colloquies may have been enhanced by the fact that the discussants were drawing inspiration not from standardized textbooks, but from syllabuses of original works: literary texts, political disputation, scientific papers, and the like. Hutchins's conviction that the great books of the Western tradition constituted a major resource of general-education doubtless encouraged this pedagogic practice of challenging the student directly with important intellectual texts. Kenneth Murdock, when chairman of the Committee on General Education at Harvard, once remarked that a major difference between general education at Harvard and at Chicago was that every Harvard student read *Moby Dick* and every Chicago student read Thucydides. One Chicago College faculty member during those years was inclined to accept the accuracy of at least the second half of Murdock's remark. He listened to two young men, sitting on the C-bench in front of Cobb Hall, arguing about the origin of an attractive and exotic-looking girl who was passing by. "I tell you, she's a Peloponnesian," one was overheard to say.

The vitality of the four-year general-education College was dependent upon early admission—that is, upon attracting to the University a substantial number of students who had completed only two years of high school. Hutchins and his advisers had made a bold attempt to carve out a domain for general education by amalgamating the last two years of conventional high school and the first two years of a four-year college. But it proved difficult to persuade parents and high school advisers to send sixteen-year-olds off to Chicago. For a time the difficulty was masked by the influx of returning World War II veterans, many of them attracted by the flexibility inherent in the system of placement tests. But by the early 1950s, it became apparent that the flow of early entrants was insufficient to ensure the future of the College. Accordingly, in 1953, under President Lawrence Kimpton, the University moved to a collegiate four-year pattern roughly similar to that which prevailed during the first decade of the Hutchins administration. This combined a substantial portion of the

Clarence Faust

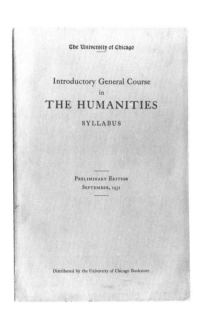

Proposed master plan for the College of the University, 1927

existing general-education program with the opportunity for undergraduate concentrations in the four divisions, as well as for senior-year
optional study in some of the professional schools.

Just as the general-education college of 1942–53 was built
upon the internal conversations of the preceding twenty years, so the
subsequent course of undergraduate education at Chicago reflects the
experience of that seminal decade. Students and faculty members
continue to debate over what knowledge is most worth having, and
how one goes about getting it. Institutional adjustments and curricular
inventions have aimed at clarifying and improving both the general-
education and the specialized portions of the curriculum. Collegiate
divisions matching the four graduate divisions were set up to provide
loci for academic interchange and joint program planning. A fifth
unit, the New Collegiate Division, was commissioned to undertake
interdisciplinary ventures. In the sciences, opportunities for undergraduate research proliferated. Even the persistent problem of improving students' writing skills received sympathetic and sensible attention
from the College. The renovation of Harper Library as the College's
focus, and the establishment of the adjacent undergraduate library as a
reading and study center, evidenced continuing commitment to the
tasks set by President Burton.

Robert Maynard Hutchins at his
inauguration

The Hutchins Years

No man can come to the presidency of the University of Chicago without being awed by the University and its past. From the moment of its founding it took its place among the notable institutions of the earth. Through four administrations it has held its course, striving to attain the ideals established at the beginning and coming closer toward its goal each year. . . . The guaranty of its future is the devotion and ability of these men and women, who have set their mark upon the University, so that whatever changes in organization may come, its spirit will be the same. That spirit has been characterized by emphasis on productive scholarship, by emphasis on men before everything else, on work with and for Chicago, and on an experimental attitude. And these four characteristics will, I think, be the insignia of the University's spirit to the end.

— Robert Maynard Hutchins

H utchins was the youngest person elected to the presidency of Chicago and the longest to hold that office. Young, handsome, eloquent, he quickly became a formidable figure on the national educational scene. Hutchins of Chicago was often quoted in the press; people even knew his middle name. In his inaugural address of November 19, 1929, he praised the "experimental attitude" of the University of Chicago as one of its defining characteristics. It is the experimental attitude of Hutchins that remains the most memorable aspect of his influential presidency.

A hallmark of these years was a tireless quest for organizational changes that would stimulate greater intellectual contact among the various units of the University, which would generate what Hutchins sometimes described as "the great conversation." An early move was to place the traditional departmental units within a new administrative structure. In 1930, the University was reorganized into five

President and Mrs. Hutchins

divisions: Biological Sciences, Humanities, Physical Sciences, Social Sciences, and the College. Together with the professional schools, these divisions provided the structure of the University. Many budgetary and administrative functions hitherto performed in the President's office were invested in the deans of the divisions and schools. The four-year general-education College, as it took shape, was organized, not departmentally, but by functional teaching staffs. With the alteration and obliteration of many traditional boundaries of academic separation, one older Chicagoan was reminded of the title of E. P. Roe's once-popular novel about the Chicago fire, *Barriers Burned Away*.

This disposition to test the limits of the established disciplines was also seen in the invention of committees and institutes to engage in interdisciplinary teaching and research. Cooperative research, such as the work done under the auspices of the Social Science Research Committee, had been carried on at the University for some years. Initially, such cooperation was confined to closely related subject areas. However, Hutchins's 1930 reorganization led to more vigorous exploration of innovative academic combinations. By the end of the 1940s, interdisciplinary committees in the Social Sciences had been organized in such areas as Human Development, Social Thought, Race Relations, and Communications. Simultaneously, in Humanities, there emerged committees in History of Culture, Ideas and Methods, and Comparative Literature. The Divinity School developed new programs dealing with relationships between religion and the arts, social issues, and psychology. In the sciences, the Research Institutes drew together investigators from many fields. In fact, by the early 1950s, the allure of the interdisciplinary was so pervasive on the Quadrangles that it was said some people committed interdisciplinary acts without being aware that they were being tempted to do so.

Human Development, one of the earliest of the interdisciplinary committees, provided an apt example of what was involved in developing these fresh perspectives. Established in 1940 as an outgrowth of the earlier Committee on Child Development, Human Development drew faculty and students from both the Biological Sciences and Social Sciences. What Human Development undertook to study was revealed in a memorandum from Mandel Sherman of the Orthogenic School to Ralph Tyler, the first Chairman of Human Development:

Ralph Tyler

We might, for example, choose the general problem of frustration because we have a body of knowledge about it and because there are many assumptions upon which to base further experimentation.... If an experiment in frustration would be set up, we would like to evaluate the effect of different social experiences upon

Frank Knight

John U. Nef, Jr., left, with Charles Moraze,
a visitor to the University

On following pages: Great Books
Seminar led by Mortimer Adler, 1947

University of Chicago Round Table
program on "Censorship," January
18, 1942. Left to right are H. D.
Lasswell, Byron Price, and William
Benton.

President Robert M. Hutchins with
students participating in the Two-Year
High School Entrants' Program, 1943

the frustrability of normal and neurotic children, the effect of physical and nutritional defects and deficiencies upon the ease with which a child can be emotionally disturbed and frustrated, and the meaning of the various early undesirable experiences and traumas in producing varying degrees of reactivity to a frustration situation. Thus, the problem would necessitate a very intimate relationship between a nutritionist, child psychologist, sociologist, pediatrician, and educationist.

A similar broad sweep across divisional boundaries was envisaged by John U. Nef, Jr., an economics historian, who was disturbed by increasing specialization and the apparent divergence of ·scientific and humanistic modes of inquiry. In discussions with Robert Redfield, an anthropologist, Frank Knight, an economist, and Hutchins, Nef laid the groundwork for the Committee on Social Thought, whose roster of distinguished members included art historians, novelists, and philosophers, as well as social scientists. Social Thought also brought to the Quadrangles, for lectures and seminars, notable figures in the arts, letters, and sciences.

Of the interdisciplinary committees created between 1930 and 1950, some have remained active in roles substantially similar to those they took on half a century ago. Some transformed themselves into departments: the former Committee on Statistics is now the Department of Statistics, and Human Development is a core element of the Department of Psychology. And in some cases committees faded away as members turned to pursue other interests or discovered other venues for their work. The committees also attracted to Chicago a number of scholars who, while strongly committed to a committee program, also gave new strength to a related department.

Hutchins's advocacy of study programs based upon the classic texts, which came to be known as the Great Books, challenged conventional compartmentation in the academy. The works were chosen as notable illuminations of persistent human problems, from the writings of philosophers, artists, and scientists. A major presupposition underlying the study of these major works, whether undertaken in school and college or among adult groups, was that the discussion these books stimulated led to a more mature understanding of present-day issues, while at the same time sharpening the students' skills as readers and thinkers.

As the Great Books movement demonstrated, the Hutchins administration saw a renewed commitment to adult education. The University established an educational radio series in the 1930s—the University of Chicago Round Table—which for many years commanded an enthusiastic national audience. Even more ambitious ventures in public education were the Commission on the Freedom of the Press and the Committee to Frame a World Constitution.

Controversy swirled around many of Hutchins's actions and views—something which would come as no surprise to a careful reader of the Great Books. Indeed, sometimes the vigor of the presidential rhetoric seemed calculated to stir up any slumbering opposition. The greatest public outcry of these years came when intercollegiate football was abolished in 1939, as it became obvious that the University could no longer compete against schools that lavishly subsidized athletics. Responses to the abandonment of football ranged from disappointment to hysteria among sportswriters, some alumni, and passionate fans in the general public. Other alumni and most educators found the decision radical but rational. One individual, presumably in agreement with the decision, suggested that the University replace football with bullfighting: "Thrills, excitement, merriment, danger, horsemanship, suspense. A test of man's cunning vs. bull courage." A decade later Hutchins amusedly remarked, "I greatly fear that my administration will be remembered solely because it was the one in which intercollegiate football was abolished." A minor irony of these experimental years was that Chicago's last coach, while serving as an adviser to the coaching staff of the Chicago Bears, revolutionized professional football by reintroducing the T-formation.

RELATIVE IMPORTANCE OF TWO ANNOUNCEMENTS

*West stands of Stagg Field—site of the
first controlled, self-sustaining nuclear
chain reaction*

December 2, 1942, and Postwar Research

R esearch in the physical sciences reached a momentous stage in the 1940s with the harnessing of atomic energy. Perhaps no other field of inquiry has demonstrated so graphically—and with such implications that cut across so many areas of human activity—the importance of basic scientific research as that which led to the first controlled nuclear chain reaction, which took place at the University on December 2, 1942.

The discovery of fission—the splitting of the uranium atom—had been achieved in Berlin in 1939. Believing that German scientists were likely to turn the discovery into a weapon of war, Leo Szilard and Eugene Wigner prevailed upon Albert Einstein to sign his now-famous letter to President Roosevelt warning of the danger to mankind if the Nazis could produce a nuclear bomb first. At Roosevelt's direction, the Advisory Committee on Uranium was established in Washington, D.C., to assess the scientific possibilities of fission. One of the committee's first acts was to allocate $6,000 in 1940 to buy pure graphite bricks—perhaps the first case on record of government support of nuclear research.

With the graphite, Enrico Fermi, who had fled Fascist Italy shortly after receiving the Nobel Prize in 1938, started a series of small physics experiments at Columbia University. He developed the exponential pile, a forerunner of the chain-reacting pile, to measure the neutron multiplication properties associated with various arrangements of graphite and uranium oxide. Writing of these experiments, the Chicago physicist Robert Sachs noted, "It quickly became apparent that a rather large scale effort would be needed to obtain the required amounts of materials (graphite and uranium oxide) and to insure that they were pure enough."

Enrico Fermi

This larger effort was mounted at Chicago. The Metallurgical Laboratory had been established on December 6, 1941, the day before Pearl Harbor, by the Office of Scientific Research and Development and by Arthur Holly Compton, a Nobel laureate and Professor of Physics at the University. Compton had become a major figure in the effort to coordinate scientific research on fission as chairman of the National Academy of Sciences committee responsible for war research. He judged Fermi's experiments to be important enough to decide to coordinate the project himself. Early in 1942, Compton suggested that the chain-reaction program be centralized in Chicago; in April, Fermi and several of his associates took up residence at International House on the University campus.

The original plan was to build the pile at Argonne, a remote locale outside Chicago in the Cook County Forest Preserve. However, construction workers for the contractor had gone out on strike, threatening a serious delay. Fermi went to Compton and told him of an alternative site: the squash court beneath the west stands of Stagg Field where the Metallurgical Lab had already built several small exponential piles. After Fermi described the safety controls he proposed for the chain-reacting pile, Compton gave his approval on the basis of Fermi's controls and his reputation as a careful experimenter. Writing later of the incident, Compton explained:

We did not see how a true nuclear explosion could possibly occur, but the amount of potentially radioactive material present in the pile would be enormous, and anything that would cause excessive ionizing radiation in such a location would be intolerable. . . . According to every rule of organizational protocol, I should have taken the matter to my superior. But this would have been unfair. President Hutchins was in no position to make an independent judgment of the hazards involved. Based on considerations of the university's welfare, the only answer he could have given would have been no. And this answer would have been wrong. So I assumed the responsibility myself.

When Compton reported his decision to General Leslie Groves, the officer in charge of the Manhattan Project, and others in Washington, "faces went white," but he was not told to stop. "The element of risk was accepted as a hazard of war."

Chicago Pile One, or CP-1, was built under the supervision of Walter Zinn and Herbert Anderson. Construction began on Monday morning, November 16, 1942. In a matter of weeks, nearly 800,000 pounds of graphite were machined into lattice sections and 22,000 pieces of uranium oxide pressed into the required shapes. A crew of graduate students, professors, and hired laborers put in ninety-hour weeks to finish the pile.

On December 2, Fermi was ready to carry out his test. The morning was devoted to preliminary measurements. "The serious work began after lunch," Anderson recalled. Fermi ordered all but one of the cadmium rods unlocked and removed. Then he asked that the

The atomic pile under construction beneath Stagg Field stands

last rod be set at one of the earlier morning locations. When the measurement checked out with his calculations, he directed that the rod be moved to the last setting. "This is going to do it," Fermi told Compton, ordering the safety or "zip" rod withdrawn. "Now it will become self-sustaining. The trace [on the recorder] will climb and continue to climb; it will not level off."

The neutron intensity kept climbing every fraction of a second. Soon the recording pen was off-scale. The scale was changed, the pen returned to a point near zero, and the experiment was resumed. With the intensity rising exponentially—as Fermi had predicted—the scale had to be changed again. By this time, though, some onlookers were "a little nervous," said Anderson, since they were aware that left uncontrolled the pile would build up an enormous charge, risking a possibility that had not yet entered the scientists' vocabulary, a "meltdown."

But Fermi pushed ahead, withholding the safety rod for a few more critical seconds in order to prove that the pile had achieved a self-sustaining reaction. After a total elapsed time of four and a half minutes, he gave the order, "Zip in." Zinn released his rope and the control rod went in with a bang. The intensity measure abruptly fell off to a comfortable level. "Then there was a small cheer," Anderson reported. "The experiment was a success."

Fermi and his colleagues became intimately involved in the ensuing program that led to the development of the nuclear bomb, both at the Argonne site, which was completed in 1943, and at Los Alamos, where Fermi moved in September 1944. At the end of the war there was prompt attention to the implications of these consequential applications of nuclear research for what might lie ahead in peacetime scientific inquiry.

Recognizing that for the most part the scientists involved in the Manhattan Project did not hold regular appointments, and aiming to maintain the concentration of prominent physical scientists brought to Chicago by the wartime emergency, the University set up three institutes devoted to the study of nuclear physics. Through the establishment of the Institute for Nuclear Studies (now the Enrico Fermi Institute), the Institute of Metals (now the James Franck Institute), and the Institute of Radiology and Biophysics (later part of the Committee on Biophysics), the University also hoped to ensure that the habits of secrecy made necessary by the war would not continue in peacetime and inhibit freedom of investigation.

To discuss the political and ethical issues of the new situation, the University convened a conference on September 19–20,

James Franck

1945, with participants including physical scientists, philosophers, political scientists, and political leaders. There was general agreement that the explosion of the bomb had fundamentally altered the relationship between science and politics, and that the scientific community should be prepared to offer guidance for a serious rethinking of national and international policy on these matters. One immediate concern was the threat of military restrictions on the flow of technical information; according to many experts, this would impede atomic research and eventually pose a security threat to the nation. Fermi, unable to attend the conference, sent his views on the issue to Hutchins.

Secrecy on the scientific phases of the development would not only be of little effect but soon would hamper the progress of nuclear physics in this country to such an extent as to even make it exceedingly difficult to grasp the importance of new discoveries made elsewhere in this field.

Willard F. Libby

In response to this fear, the Atomic Scientists of Chicago, organized by Eugene Rabinowitch and James Franck, lobbied Congress for legislation to protect freedom of research. Hutchins committed $10,000 of University funds to help the cause. In December 1945, the group started *The Bulletin of the Atomic Scientists*, a newsletter devoted to exploring the problems of the atomic age. (As its symbol the group chose the "clock of doom," the image of a clock face with its hands set a few minutes before midnight.) Meanwhile, other members of the faculty assisted in drafting federal legislation to place nuclear research in civilian hands. Much of the McMahon Atomic Energy Control Act of 1946 was written in the basement of the old Law School.

In announcing the formation of the Research Institutes, Hutchins underscored the University's commitment to redirecting atomic energy through research in chemistry, physics, basic materials, and medicine. He reported that the institutes would be financed chiefly through the University's own resources in an effort "to advance knowledge and not primarily to develop the military or industrial applications of nuclear research." He pointed out that "for the past six years the United States has abandoned both basic research and the training of a new generation of scientists. It is essential to our progress and our welfare that we overcome that deficiency."

The Research Institutes made the University a powerful presence in postwar physical science. Concentrated in Chicago for the time being was an outstanding staff including not only Fermi and Harold C. Urey, both Nobel Prize laureates, but also Edward Teller, Herbert Anderson, Cyril S. Smith, Philip Schutz, Maria Goeppert Mayer, Joseph Mayer, and many promising younger scientists. Institute members were appointed jointly in either the Departments of Physics or Chemistry; this greatly strengthened these departments and attracted top-flight graduate students to the programs. Students included subsequent Nobel Prize winners Murray Gell-Mann, Owen Chamberlain, T.-D. Lee, and C. N. Yang.

The first Director of the Institute for Nuclear Studies was Samuel K. Allison, who had studied physics with Robert A. Millikan and received his Ph.D. in chemistry from the University in 1923. Under Allison's and Fermi's supervision, the University constructed an advanced "atom smasher" (synchrocyclotron) inside the Accelerator Building at 56th Street and Ellis Avenue. In trial runs conducted by Herbert Anderson and John Marshall in 1951, deuterons, the nuclei of heavy hydrogen atoms, were accelerated to an energy of 250 million electron volts, the highest known energy achieved artificially with atomic particles. A year later Fermi and his associates opened up the world of particle research by discovering the resonance state of protons when bombarded with pions produced by the atom smasher.

Fermi's premature death in 1954 was a blow to the program, but his vision of Chicago as a center for theoretical research endured through the efforts of others who found the atmosphere conducive to free-ranging speculation and unusual lines of inquiry. Willard Libby, for example, interested in the properties of carbon 14, established a linear relationship between the passage of time and variation in the carbon 14 content in a material. This led to the development of the carbon 14 dating technique that proved to be of tremendous importance in geological, archaeological, and anthropological research. Similarly venturesome was Harold Urey's research into the origins of the elements, the Earth, the Moon, and the Solar System. Urey devised methods for measuring temperatures as they existed in the oceans of past geological ages from the isotope ratio in the calcium carbonate in marine fossils.

Establishment of the Argonne National Laboratory rounded out the University's pioneering role in nuclear physics. This was set up in 1946 as one of three national laboratories and was operated under contract by the University of Chicago. A permanent site for this research center was set aside on a 3,700-acre tract in Du Page County, twenty miles southwest of Chicago. When the Atomic Energy Commission replaced the Manhattan Project as the agency responsible for nuclear research, Argonne assumed major responsibilities in the field of nuclear power reactors. Since then the laboratory, with a staff of more than three thousand employees, has had a primary mission to develop the peaceful use of nuclear power.

Nobel laureates Tsung-Dao Lee and
Chen Ning Yang, 1957

Argonne National Laboratory construction

Hyde Park Urban Renewal

I n 1888, the executive secretary of the American Baptist Education Society had asserted that there was "not to be found another city in which such an institution as we need could be established, or if established could be maintained and enlarged, or if maintained could achieve wide influence or retain supremacy among us." From the start, Chicago was an urban university. Not only did the city provide support for the institution, but the city became a subject for intense scholarship and a context for the University's involvement with the community. Thus, when the University discovered after World War II that its neighborhood was undergoing rapid change, the situation became a catalyst for action.

The conditions of an aging inner city—deteriorating infrastructure, pressure for living space, inadequate city services, crime—pressed against the Quadrangles. In 1949, a group of residents organized an effort to meet these insistent problems. The goal of the Hyde Park-Kenwood Community Conference was to establish "a stabilized integrated community of high standards." While the group had no official connection with the University, faculty and staff were prominent among its membership.

When Lawrence Kimpton (1951–60) succeeded Hutchins as Chancellor of the University, the problems of the community had gone from pressing to urgent. Crime was on the rise. Unscrupulous realtors were using racial fear to "churn" houses for quick turnover and large profit. More significant than racial composition, though, were the changes in economic and social status that came about in the wake of World War II. Voter registration statistics disclosed high transience rates among the black residents moving in. The Kenwood and Woodlawn neighborhoods were especially vulnerable. As "blockbusters" got hold of the houses, one after another single-family dwellings were split up into rooming houses for the very poor.

Perhaps inevitably, in view of the magnitude of the changes in the neighborhood, there were reports that the University was con-

Lawrence Kimpton

sidering a move to a less exigent environment, perhaps to suburban Du Page County near the Argonne Laboratory, perhaps to Wisconsin near the Yerkes Observatory. Prospective mergers with other universities—Northwestern, even Stanford—were topics of speculation. Some color may have been given to these reports by the fact that the College, with some of its students as early entrants under the age of eighteen, was exploring alternative locations for a number of its courses.

The fact that the University was here to stay in Hyde Park and committed to the rehabilitation of the neighborhood was underscored on March 27, 1952. In a community meeting at Mandel Hall, Chancellor Kimpton assumed the leadership of the "Committee of Five," which led to the formation of a permanent action agency, the South East Chicago Commission. Kimpton was named president of the s.e.c.c., and Julian Levi, a Chicago lawyer, became executive director. The University underwrote a large part of the budget, with additional funds coming from area businessmen and the Field Foundation.

Enforcement of the city housing code became a major objective of the new organization. Cases of illegal conversion were documented and forwarded to city authorities for prosecution. Narcotics trafficking was another concern. One hotel near 47th Street was notorious as a drug den, with police records showing 119 arrests in and around the building in a single year. The South East Chicago Commission wrote to the owners asking whether they condoned such conduct. When the letter was ignored, Don Blakiston, a criminologist on the s.e.c.c. staff, went to work, according to a contemporary report:

He checked the narcotics bureau of the police department and painstakingly copied the police records of the hotel residents. Sixty-three had records with a total of 596 arrests. Armed with this information s.e.c.c. asked the company who insured the building if this was the sort of property it considered a good risk. The insurance was promptly canceled. This caused the bank to call its $75,000 mortgage. The hotel is now under new ownership and is operating respectably.

Simultaneously with its attention to code enforcement, the commission drew up a plan for the physical rehabilitation of Hyde Park. This involved the commercial hub centered at 55th Street and Lake Park Avenue and extending south to 57th Street. Twenty-two taverns lined 55th Street; a hodgepodge of good and bad buildings spilled out from the side streets. Urban Renewal Project No. 1, Hyde Park A and B, called for the razing of 47.3 acres of property between 52nd and 57th Streets along the west side of the Illinois Central Rail-

Julian H. Levi

University President Lawrence Kimpton, right, greets Chicago Mayor Richard J. Daley at a meeting of the South East Chicago Commission, 1956

road. In addition, properties along 55th Street would be cleared from the railroad to Ridgewood Court. In all, 150 businesses and more than 1,200 families would be relocated.

When this process began in 1953, urban renewal was a largely untested proposition. New laws on the city, state, and federal level had to be enacted to clear the way for a project of this magnitude. An important first step was made when Mayor Martin H. Kennelly designated Hyde Park as a pilot project in his citywide redevelopment program. Following the approval of a bill in Springfield providing for the acquisition of "blighted" land under the powers of eminent domain, the Chicago Land Clearance Commission began the tedious procedure of acquiring title to the buildings and clearing the land in preparation for sale to private developers.

The Federal Housing Act of 1954 was a national response to the kind of deterioration identified in Hyde Park. The law permitted federal funds to be used for the private rebuilding of urban areas (prior

55th Street in Hyde Park before demolition, 1950s

55th Street after renovation, 1960s

to the law, federal housing money could be used only for slum clearance). Kimpton, Levi, and members of the Law School faculty were
involved in drafting the legislation. After its passage, President
Eisenhower met with University officials and singled out Hyde Park
for praise, saying it was one of the most imaginative and aggressive
examples of community renewal, offering "a new basis of hope" for
America's cities.

        With the necessary tools at hand, the project swung into
action. On May 10, 1955, a torchlight parade was held on Blackstone
Avenue to celebrate the first demolition, with Chancellor Kimpton
and Chicago's new mayor, Richard J. Daley, prominent among the
dignitaries in attendance. It took two years to acquire and clear the
land before construction began. William Zeckendorf, the New York
realtor who successfully bid on the site through his Webb and Knapp
firm, was in charge of the project. Along Harper Avenue and 55th
Street, more than 150 modern townhouses were built. They were
designed by Harry Weese and carried the then-hefty sales price of
$35,100 to $40,500. Most of the houses were purchased by University
faculty and staff, with a number of families moving back to Hyde Park
from the suburbs. University Apartments, a midrise complex circum-
navigated by 55th Street, was developed for junior faculty and others
of more modest means. Designed by I. M. Pei, the modern, concrete-
faced building was presented as a "dynamic new living center," complete with underground garage and oval-shaped plaza. Two-bedroom
apartments started at $175 a month.

5111 Cornell Avenue house demolition

        The old commercial hub was reconfigured to conform
to the demands of the automobile. Lake Park Avenue, a north-south
street that ran a half block west of the railroad, was enlarged and
moved eastward to accommodate several acres of parking for the new
shopping district. The latter was a departure from the community's
scattered retailing, since it brought together a miscellany of merchan-
disers with the Hyde Park Co-op supermarket as a central store. When
it was opened, a brochure called it one of the earliest examples of a
"California-style" shopping center in Chicago.

        Stage two of Hyde Park renewal proceeded with a commu-
nity conservation plan for the area bounded by 47th Street on the
north, the Midway on the south, Cottage Grove Avenue on the west,
and Lake Michigan on the east, exclusive of the original renewal
projects and the University campus. Although less wholesale clearance
was proposed than in the previous project, the second phase ran into
stiff opposition and eventually involved a compromise over public
housing before it was ratified by the Chicago City Council in 1958.

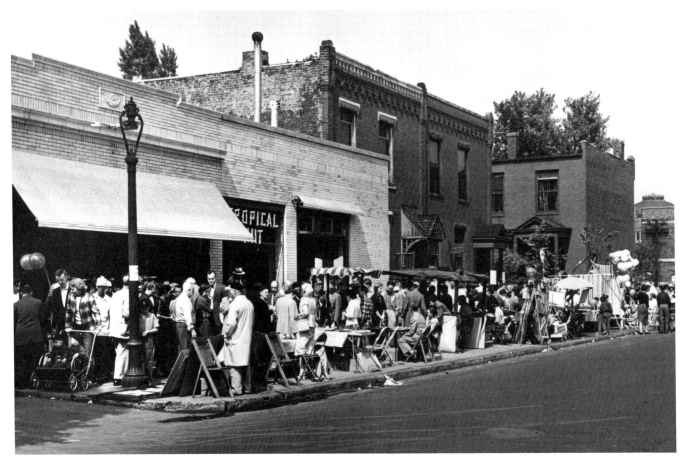

57th Street Art Fair, 1953

There would be 20 percent demolition, displacing of 4,528 families, and construction of new housing for 2,350 families. Fifty-fifth Street was widened all the way to Cottage Grove Avenue. Thirty-six acres of parks, playgrounds, and green space were added to enhance the environment and thin out the population. The University purchased property south of 55th Street between Cottage Grove and Ellis avenues from a private redevelopment corporation. Other institutions received land for their facilities, including the Chicago College of Osteopathy.

In October 1961, nine years after the mass meeting at Mandel Hall, Levi presented a progress report to the Board of Trustees:

The Urban Renewal Program has already stimulated private construction in the area. Within the past month, two apartment-house projects, one at 49th and Lake Shore Drive and the other at 54th and Hyde Park Boulevard, have been financed and announced. Total new private investment here is close to $15 million. The vote of confidence in the market place by both investors and prospective tenants is impressive.

It is a fair statement that the program to date has: (a) marshaled public investment of more than $47 million, (b) marshaled private investment, already made or committed, of more than $35 million, with additional potential private and institutional investment (exclusive of the University of Chicago) of more than $60 million, and (c) achieved a degree of community stability which could not have been anticipated a decade ago. Of course there are the Georgetowns and the Beacon Hills where processes of decay have been reversed, but the scale of Hyde Park-Kenwood is far larger and more significant.

The consequences of the urban renewal effort remain evident today everywhere in Hyde Park. The planners believed that they had saved the community by arresting in midcourse a twenty-five-year cycle of deterioration before private development on its own would have stimulated revival. They cited many impressive statistics supporting their assessment, including the fact that after 1960, Hyde Park real estate began appreciating in value, reversing the trend of disinvestment and depreciation in the inner city that was especially troublesome on Chicago's South Side. On the other hand, critics argued that the project had been unnecessarily disruptive, that the wholesale demolition of the 55th Street area had taken something important out of the neighborhood and replaced it with sterile buildings and green but useless spaces. They also asserted that more should have been done to help the community's disadvantaged, giving rise to the remark, attributed to Mike Nichols, that in Hyde Park it was "blacks and whites united to keep out the poor." What may have been forgotten in later assessments was the historical context—that forty years ago, as one of the nation's first renewal efforts, conceived and executed under trying circumstances, the Hyde Park project seemed as likely to fail as to succeed. By its own objectives, it had succeeded.

Tot Lot at 5600 Drexel Avenue

The Laird Bell Law Quadrangle

The Environment Enlivened

"Wandering in the University of Chicago today," architect Eero Saarinen wrote in the November 1960 issue of *Architectural Record*,

one is amazed at the beauty achieved by spaces surrounded by buildings all in one discipline and made out of a uniform material; where each building is being considerate of the next, and each building—through its common material—is aging in the same way. One is now far enough removed from the fight against eclecticism to admire the largeness of vision of the time, and one becomes interested in finding out how all this came about.

On one campus court, Saarinen was surprised to discover that the buildings shaping the Quadrangle had been designed by three different architects over a number of years, yet they had achieved a harmonious whole by following the Gothic style of Henry Ives Cobb. "Imagine," Saarinen injected half-humorously, "what would have happened if three or four equally eminent architects of our day were asked to do the four sides of a square!"

The architectural world had undergone fundamental changes, however, since the days of Cobb. No longer were buildings inspired by memories of Oxford colleges; indeed, the whole "neo-Gothic" fascination with spires, gargoyles, and monastic adornment was disparaged as anachronistic and phony—"false stage scenery of a bygone era," as Saarinen put it—while the clean, functional lines of Ludwig Mies van der Rohe and other modernists had become the dominant mode. The challenge facing University planners was to integrate the contemporary impulses of architecture within the tradition of the campus without disrupting a sense of unity. The noncommittal design of the Administration Building (1947), which pleased neither modernist nor traditionalist nor most laymen's eyes, was just the sort of visual muddle that persuaded the Board of Trustees, fearful of piecemeal corruption of the campus, to give Eero Saarinen responsibility for organizing a master campus plan.

Alton Linford, right, dean of the School of Social Service Administration 1956–69, with Ludwig Mies van der Rohe

Following the lean years of the Depression and the shortages of the war, the 1950s were a period of intense physical development made possible by a capital campaign. The University program called for the expenditure of nearly $60 million in new campus construction between 1954 and 1964, the largest in the institution's history. Saarinen worked closely with the Board of Trustees in two important areas before his death in 1961: preparing a master plan for campus expansion over the next decade or so and developing criteria to help architects design individual buildings that would be in accord.

The architect must make a conscientious effort to develop a mass which is sympathetic and enhancing to the total mass developed by the older buildings. High-rise towers, so fashionable today, may spoil a skyline which was beautiful. The scale and dominance of vertical or horizontal in surrounding buildings has a great bearing on what characteristic a new building should have. If the character of the university or of the immediate neighbors is, for instance, a vertical one, then verticality should be expressed.

Saarinen's first master plan was presented at a joint meeting of the Trustees' Area Committee and Committee on Campus Development in 1955. It contained a blueprint for the development of the south campus, the block-deep frontage along 60th Street between Cottage Grove and Stony Island Avenues. The architect also proposed a series of "activity clusters," inspired by Cobb's concept of the self-contained inward-looking quadrangle, but diverging significantly from his rigid rectangular layout. The plan also took into account the pressing need to expand living accommodations for College students. The first postwar residence hall, Woodward Court, designed by Saarinen and opened in 1958, was located north of Ida Noyes Hall. This residence and dining hall for undergraduate women was a straightforward structure, the units made of reinforced concrete and faced with limestone. Two years later Stanley R. Pierce Hall, a residence for undergraduate men, was completed at the corner of University Avenue and 55th Street. Pierce Hall, a concrete tower clad with limestone bay windows and brick siding, was designed by Harry Weese, the architect commissioned to design the townhouses for the Hyde Park urban renewal project.

Saarinen's design of the Laird Bell Quadrangle for the Law School was a striking departure from precedent. The complex was focused on the law library where black glass walls, seemingly pleated, created a dramatic effect facing the Midway. Saarinen explained that his purpose was to fit the building comfortably between the Gothic Burton-Judson Residence Halls on the west and the contemporary American Bar Center on the east. "By stressing a small, broken scale,

Woodward Court residence hall

Pierce Hall

Frank Lloyd Wright's Robie House

Center for Continuing Education

a lively silhouette and especially verticality in the library design, we intended to make it a good neighbor with the neo-Gothic dormitories," he said.

Similar answers to the institutional needs of the south campus made 60th Street a laboratory for varied concepts of modern design. Edward Durell Stone's Center for Continuing Education, for example, introduced a geometric recessed pattern on the seventy-two exterior columns in an effort to reintroduce decoration into architecture. The Charles Stewart Mott Industrial Relations Center, designed by Schmidt, Garden, & Erickson, used aluminum curtain-wall construction with limestone walls at each end. In 1963, ground was broken for the School of Social Service Administration. The Mies van der Rohe design followed the architect's trademark pattern of steel-ribbed glass rectangles, this time flung across a "weightless" horizontal plane rather than the verticals of his famous skyscrapers.

By most accounts, the new architecture was found to be compatible with the Gothic under the sensitive and carefully articulated master plan. The most stringent lines of the modernists were softened, while the advantages of postwar breakthroughs in the use of interior space for laboratories, classrooms, and dormitories were exploited to the full. The happy coincidence of old and new would have suffered a tremendous setback, however, were it not for the efforts of the University and interested citizens to save Frank Lloyd Wright's Robie House. This low-slung building, designed for industrialist Frederick Robie in 1908, was a prime example of Wright's Prairie House design, and anticipated by several decades concepts of residential design and convenience. Among its pioneering ideas were a trilevel floor plan, use of steel beams in construction, a three-car garage, family room, and indirect cove lighting. "Almost every house built in America today owes some of its ideas to the Robie House," said an architectural critic.

With the Robie House threatened with possible demolition, a fundraising drive was initiated. In 1963, the University agreed to assume title to the property and responsibility for its upkeep, including restoration of the two main rooms. Today Wright's masterpiece, at the corner of 58th Street and Woodlawn Avenue, is a popular tourist attraction and draws thousands of visitors a year.

As the decision to give priority to the construction of Woodward Court and Pierce Tower suggested, the physical reshaping of the campus responded to needs created by expanding student enrollment. Between 1955 and 1965, following the relocation of the bachelor's degree to the normal four-year plan after high school, the number of

College students nearly doubled, from 1,350 to 2,351. Although the Chicago College had never been primarily a commuter institution, the post-1955 influx represented an even more decisive movement toward a national student population. Of the 674 first-year students entering in the fall of 1964, for example, 65 percent were from outside Illinois; they arrived from forty-five states and five foreign countries, with nearly as many of them from the New York City area as from Chicago.

At the same time, increased enrollment in the graduate divisions and the professional schools boosted the demand for more student housing. Recognizing the problem early, Kimpton undertook an aggressive program to purchase existing neighborhood properties for conversion to undergraduate and graduate student use. Because University-owned housing was exempt from local property taxes, upgrading of the buildings was possible even at below-market rental rates. According to one report by University planners:

The program for married students began slowly in 1955 and 1956 and accelerated from 1961 until its culmination in 1966. It involved 47 separate parcels of property with a combined book value of over $14 million. All the properties except Phemister Hall were purchased and renovated, not built.

It was recognized, of course, that in addition to attractive and convenient student housing, there was a need for additional centers of social and cultural activity, stronger support facilities, and improved amenities in the existing residential halls. In 1964, these needs were canvassed by a faculty committee chaired by Walter J. Blum of the Law School. The committee centered its attention on the northern portion of the campus, between 57th and 55th Streets, and, with the advice of the architect, Edward Larrabee Barnes, recommended the creation of a number of interrelated facilities.

Over the years important elements of the Blum committee's program have been realized. One was the Cochrane-Woods Art Center, established in 1973. Made possible by a grant from the Woods Charitable Fund, the multipurpose building housed a lecture hall, classrooms, and library facilities. It shared a sculpture courtyard with the new David and Alfred Smart Museum of Art. Nearby, a few years later, appeared the new home for the Court Theatre. In cultural matters the writ of the Blum committee ran even south of 57th Street. The Music Department, which had suffered—but not in silence— many years of substandard housing, was relocated in Goodspeed Hall and equipped with larger practice rooms and a splendid recital hall. And venerable Mandel Hall, site of occasional concerts by the Chicago

Discus thrower Catherine Vanderloos, 1974

Football team plays Oberlin, 1973

Symphony Orchestra since 1903, was restored to first-class condition
in 1981 with the support of the Regenstein Foundation.

These facilities enhanced the range of extracurricular opportunities. Similarly, the renovation of the Henry Crown Field House
and the development of new athletic areas—a track and playing
fields—west of Ellis Avenue further stimulated already lively programs
of intramural and intercollegiate sports. By 1979, the Board of Athletics counted a total of forty-eight intramural activities, and observed
cautiously that the program "may well be unique among colleges
in the country in the extent to which it engages students."

For three decades after the University withdrew from
intercollegiate football, Maroon athletes continued to compete, at the
small-college level, in many other sports, although the highly pub-
licized exodus from the gridiron tended to mask this fact. Chicago
teams made especially creditable showings in swimming and in basketball. Even here success was kept in proportion; the star center of an
excellent basketball team in the late 1950s insisted on moving out of

his fraternity house because, he said, too much talk about basketball interfered with his studying. The University of Chicago Track Club, under the direction of Coach Ted Haydon, became a home away from home for many amateur athletes of great talent, including some Olympians.

After 1960, Chicago edged in a gingerly fashion back toward the football field, first with an informal class and then with varsity competition in 1969. Within a few years it had joined the Midwest Collegiate Athletic Conference, playing against many of the same colleges the Maroons had encountered in other sports since leaving the Big Ten. Then, in 1986, Chicago withdrew from the Midwest Conference and joined with other private research universities in organizing the University Athletic Association, which features high-spirited (and high-minded) competition in all major sports. An equally important development of the past two decades has been the expansion of intercollegiate varsity competition for women students.

This summary account of changes in the educational environment opened with a reference to Saarinen's tribute to the beauty of the Quadrangles. Perhaps it can close by pointing to two additional ways in which the eye of the beholder was prompted to find delight in the scene. First, distinguished works of sculpture, including Henry Moore's *Nuclear Energy* on the site of the first controlled nuclear chain reaction, became focal points of attention. Second, when President George W. Beadle (1961–68) came to Chicago, he brought with him a horticulturist's solicitude for grass, shrubs, and flowers. The plantings he directed and the greenery he protected are a lasting legacy.

Sculptor Henry Moore examining his nearly-finished sculpture Nuclear Energy *in his studio in England*

The Regenstein and Crerar Libraries

I t was during the 1960s, in the years of George Beadle's presidency, Edward H. Levi's provostship, and Levi's presidency with John T. Wilson as provost, that Chicago's resurgence of academic leadership in the disciplines occurred. Levi (1968–75) reorganized the College again on something akin to the Hutchins model, and, with the success of the 1965 fundraising campaign, strengthened the faculty in many areas.

These advances could not have taken place without the continuing development of the Library's research collections. The growth of these holdings was fundamental to scholarly excellence, yet Chicago faced great institutional challenges in handling the explosion of information. The task was not simply a matter of keeping up with each year's printing of books and periodicals, but of expanding into new or previously neglected fields of research and formats of information as knowledge and specialties proliferated.

One way to give the situation some perspective was to recall that before the University opened its doors, President Harper had gone to Europe and bought the "Berlin Collection," reportedly consisting of 175,000 volumes. This purchase made the fledgling Library one of the four largest in the United States. When Harper Library was opened in 1912, its capacity was one million volumes, a then-staggering total. But half a century later, in 1962, the Library's book holdings had reached 2.2 million and were growing at an unprecedentedly rapid rate. Herman H. Fussler, Library Director, reported the accelerating pace and broadening scope of acquisitions:

The Far Eastern Library added a total of some 7,000 volumes during the year, including 2,152 volumes in Chinese and 4,625 volumes in Japanese. It is estimated that nearly 10 percent of all library book and serial expenditures were devoted, in one way or another, to Slavic and East European acquisitions during the past year.

The Map Library added a total of 4,420 sheets to its collection, bringing the total to 189,318 sheets exclusive of aerial photographs.

Regenstein Library reading room

On opposite page: At groundbreaking ceremonies for the Joseph Regenstein Library, in front from left to right, President George Beadle, Mrs. Joseph Regenstein, Joseph Regenstein, Jr., and Gaylord Donnelley

Harper Memorial Library reading room before renovation, early 1960s

The total additions to the Library during the last year numbered 82,284. This figure is an increase of about 20,000 over 1959–60; and it's an increase of an additional 10,000 over 1957–58.

Circulation was increasing just as briskly. Total circulation in 1962 was 821,246 volumes, an increase of 90,348 volumes, or 12 percent, over the prior academic year. Circulation per cardholder, including faculty and staff, averaged 161.9 volumes a year. This was almost four times the average number recorded in 1953–54 by other major university libraries.

Library books in the early 1960s were dispersed in departmental libraries or jammed into whatever space could be found in the Harper building. Infrequently used books were stored across the Midway in the basement of the Center for Continuing Education. For years plans had been discussed for new facilities to supplement Harper. A host of issues, however, had to be settled beforehand to ensure that the new quarters would meet the exacting demands of contemporary and future scholarship. One issue was whether the best approach lay in building a central library or in expanding the existing departmental libraries. The general weight of argument, supported by the Trustees, was to plan for a central library for the social sciences and humanities with a provision for a science library in the future. Location, though, was a major quandary.

Initial consideration was given to two possible sites for the central library: (1) in the area between Swift and Rosenwald Halls north of Harper, or (2) on the west side of University Avenue at 58th Street, where the tennis courts were located. Eero Saarinen's master plan was the first to suggest moving the library out of the Main Quadrangle and locating it north of 57th Street on Stagg Field. This proposal was eventually adopted, for it avoided the problem of accommodating such a massive structure within the confines of the original campus, even though it meant a departure from the principle, set forth in 1902, of connecting departmental libraries with the academic units in adjoining buildings.

Financing the new library became the top priority of the "Campaign for Chicago," a fundraising drive begun in 1965 with the goal of raising $160 million by 1975. President Beadle underscored the importance of the new graduate library, calling it "a new center of gravity" for the institution and "our primary and most urgent need." Only twenty days after the opening of the campaign, it was announced that the Joseph Regenstein Foundation, endowed by the late Chicago industrialist, would contribute $10 million for the construction of the library. There were several other large gifts for the $20.5 million building, including $500,000 from the Harriet Pullman Schermerhorn Charitable Trust, and a $3.4 million building grant from the U.S. Office of Education.

Ground was broken for the library late in 1967. The building was substantially more spacious than it appeared. With two of its seven floors underground, Regenstein Library was the largest building at the University (584,886 gross square feet), but it did not overwhelm the scale of the Quadrangles to the south. Its 150 miles of shelves held 3.5 million volumes. The building had a seating capacity of 2,897 and included 260 separate study units for assignment to faculty researchers.

Each of the major floors was divided into four elements. To the west were the book stacks. To the east were faculty studies and reading areas. Between the stacks and reading areas were staff offices and the stairways and elevators between floors. Walter Netsch, the senior architect, described the building's exterior design as contemporary, but "more Gothic" than most of the new buildings on campus. "The limestone and the articulation of the facade have given nice

Boxes of books leaving Harper Memorial Library for Regenstein Library

Movers bring boxes into the newly finished Regenstein Library

On following pages: Regenstein Library reading rooms

The John Crerar Library

scale to a large building which could have been a great ugly box,"
he observed.

At dedication ceremonies on October 31, 1970, President
Levi praised the Trustees, members of the Library staff, and others for
joining to create one of the world's great research libraries. He pointed
out that throughout history great libraries have never been "just"
libraries, but centers of learning and discussion:

They bear witness through their existence in many lands at many periods of
history to the pervasiveness of man's search for truth. The other side of the matter
is that almost every country at some time has seen the destruction of knowledge
and books, and the ouster of scholars. It is well for us to remember the glory and
the defeats, and to express the hope, in the words of the message given to the
Acton Library at Cambridge, that through knowledge there will be the substitu-
tion of freedom for force in the government of men, and that this library will
contribute to the liberation of the mind, the understanding of civility, the exalta-
tion of the spirit.

The accelerated growth of knowledge and the broadened scope of research also pointed to the need for a consolidated science library. To accommodate the needs of the physical and biological sciences, plans for a new library building were moved forward by President Hanna H. Gray (1978–present). This project was given a crucial focus in 1981, when the Board of Trustees entered into an agreement for the transfer of the independent John Crerar Library to the University from its site on the campus of the Illinois Institute of Technology. The result was the consolidation of the University's holdings of science volumes with the 650,000-volume Crerar collection. In 1982, construction began for a library to house the combined collections. When it was completed two years later, the John Crerar Library formed the centerpiece of a new Science Quadrangle situated between 57th and 58th Streets, and Ellis and Drexel avenues. The Science Quadrangle served to unify existing laboratory and teaching facilities for the science divisions, including the Cummings Life Science Center, Henry Hinds Laboratory for the Geophysical Sciences, and Samuel Kersten, Jr., Physics Teaching Center.

At present, the Library's holdings consist of more than six million volumes. Growing from the earliest book purchases of President Harper in Berlin, and augmented by modern facilities, the strength of the Library remains a key indicator of the University's commitment to basic research.

A Regenstein Library reading room

International House from the
Midway Plaisance

The Growth of International Studies

From its beginnings the University of Chicago took account of what was going on beyond the campus, the city, and the nation. Even before settling in as the first President, William Rainey Harper scoured the bookstores of Europe for volumes that became the cornerstone of the University Library. Notable scholars were recruited from centers of learning in the Old World. The Oriental Institute undertook to study the archaeological and intellectual records of the ancient Near East, and to consider the bearing of this history on the West. On the cornerstone of the original Oriental Institute building, Haskell Hall, can still be discerned the legend *Lux Ex Oriente* (Light from the East). Similarly, the frieze over the doorway of the present Oriental Institute building represents the transit of civilization from East to West, with celebrated monuments of the two cultures bracketed between figures of an Egyptian lion and an American bison.

The Columbian Exposition, coincident with the opening of the University, had a pronounced international perspective. Wags on the Quadrangles sometimes suggested that the exotic dances of Little Egypt on the Midway Plaisance had something to do with Chicago's early eminence in anthropology. More clearly, however, the Columbian Exposition featured a World's Parliament of Religions, which stirred American interest in the beliefs of non-Western peoples. This led to the establishment of two distinguished lectureships in the Divinity School—one bringing scholars of non-Western religions to Chicago, the other sending Chicago professors abroad to lecture on religion. Thus was launched a Chicago tradition of giving serious intellectual attention to religious creeds and practices different from those dominant in Europe and America. In later decades, the influential writings of historian of religions Mircea Eliade maintained and quickened this interest in the history of religions.

These early international ventures grew out of religious concerns and the conviction that the ancient Middle East was the

Mircea Eliade

cradle of Western civilization. However, political stirrings stimulated another broadening of the University's view of the world. Samuel Harper, the son of President Harper, observing the emergence of liberal political movements in czarist Russia and Slavic Eastern Europe, took the lead in promoting instruction and scholarly research in this field. He secured resources for an important expansion of the Library's Slavic holdings, as well as for a lectureship held by Thomas G. Masaryk, the political philosopher who later became first president of the Czechoslovak republic.

During the 1920s, as the quality of the University's programs became more widely recognized in foreign countries, the number of graduate and professional students from overseas increased sharply. In recognition of this influx, the Rockefeller Foundation chose Chicago as the site for International House, a center for foreign student residence and activities in the Midwest. Subsequently, the coming to power of national socialism in Germany and fascism in Italy brought to Chicago large numbers of European scholars as faculty members and graduate students. The sciences, art history, and Near Eastern philology were fields that especially profited from this movement across the Atlantic. After World War II the University repaid this intellectual debt by establishing a program that enabled Chicago professors to assist the University of Frankfurt in restoring its academic vitality.

America's rise to world leadership after the war opened new horizons for serious scholarship. The great surveying parties by which Chicago's early sociologists, political scientists, and social workers took stock of the assorted people that industrialization and urbanization had thrown together, were extended outward. Robert E. Park's 1920 description of the city "as a laboratory for the social sciences" now required amplification: in the 1950s and thereafter, the world served as a laboratory for research. Leonard D. White, a political scientist, spoke of this transformation in a paper delivered to his colleagues in 1955:

The social sciences in America have been limited to some degree by the boundaries of American life and American problems. To be forced to operate in a different culture—to have to bridge the gap between a less developed or differently developed culture and our own—is a chastening and an educational affair.

A striking example of the new ground being broken was the development of the University as a center of Asian and other non-Western studies. Anthropologist Robert Redfield's influential essay, "Thinking about a Civilization," provided intellectual grounding for several of the Chicago programs. Dissatisfied with the narrowness of

Samuel N. Harper

International House dining room

Robert Redfield

*A gathering of some of the members
of the committee for the comparative
study of New Nations*

*Participants in the Asia Lecture
Series, 1949*

most curricula designed to give students an understanding of other civilizations, Redfield proposed a broad comparative framework, combining approaches from the social sciences and the humanities, for such inquiries. "Acquaintance with a civilization is experiencing its life almost as if I myself embodied it," he wrote. "It is the more expressive utterances and representations—the autobiography, song, music, art, intimate episode and folk and popular lore and literature—that best cause my mind and feelings to enter into the minds and feelings of the carriers of that other civilization." In 1951, Redfield launched a project to study India under this comparative approach.

Other Chicago scholars were becoming interested in Asia from other vantage points. Edward Shils, a sociologist, traveled to the Continent to study the Indian educational system. Bert Hoselitz, an economic historian, did field studies in India on the effects of cultural factors in economic development. Milton Friedman studied India's economy at first hand, and prepared a critical analysis of Nehru's second five-year plan. Still others—educator Francis Chase, historian Donald Lach, geographer Gilbert White, sociologist Philip Hauser— were in Asia.

Returning to Chicago, some of them met on an informal basis to share information on their research. In 1955, they formed the Committee of South Asian Studies to give direction to this burst of interest. The committee undertook to stimulate and coordinate research activities, to prepare teaching materials, to develop advanced programs for graduate students specializing in South Asia, and to provide facilities and guidance for South Asian students.

Chicago's broad-scale approach to international studies promptly attracted national attention. Under the Sputnik-inspired National Defense Education Act, the University received funds to develop a center for South Asian studies. In 1960, the Ford Foundation announced its intention of giving substantial grants to select American universities for international and non-Western area studies. The Chicago faculty prepared a long-range plan for the development of an international center with an expanded faculty, support facilities, and library materials. The proposal gained the strong support of Chauncy D. Harris, a geographer and former Dean of Social Sciences, who acted as intermediary between the University and the foundation.

The Ford Foundation's favorable response to this plan enabled the University to create a permanent structure for international programs already under way, and to move vigorously into areas not previously covered. The Ford grant was for $5.4 million. Aside from South Asian studies, which was allotted $1.8 million, funding permit-

Albert Pick Hall for International Studies

Philip Hauser with the former president of India

ted the development of area programs dealing with Africa, Latin
America, the Far East, the Middle East, and Eastern Europe. These
related enterprises found their headquarters in the new Albert Pick
Hall for International Studies located on the Main Quadrangle.

The emphasis on international studies made itself felt
throughout the University, although it was not really true that classes
in traditional European and American topics came to be known as
"non-non-Western" courses. However, two decades before most
universities became aware of the need to enlarge the curricular pur-
view, the Chicago College instituted three year-long general education
courses dealing, respectively, with Chinese, Indic, and Islamic civilizations. In each of these courses, humanists and social scientists combined their talents to give students an understanding of how the arts,
religion, politics, economics, and social structure worked together to
form the texture of these great civilizations. A substantial grant from
the Carnegie Corporation in 1957 enabled the College to create and
staff these courses, to publish syllabi for each program, and to invite
faculty members from other colleges to come to Chicago as teaching
interns, to gain experience in ways of introducing non-Western topics
into the liberal arts curriculum.

These expanded international activities demanded close
cooperation between social scientists and humanists. They gave direct
impetus to the establishing, during the early 1960s, of three new
language-literature-civilization departments: Slavic, Far Eastern (now

East Asian), and South Asian. The Department of History ventured boldly beyond the traditional European-American concentration through a series of major appointments in non-Western fields. This movement toward a more comprehensive perspective was signaled by the publication in 1964 of William H. McNeill's *The Rise of the West*, a critical evaluation of Western civilization in light of world history.

Perhaps the most memorable instance of the interplay between serious work in a traditional discipline and a sharpened sensitivity to what was happening on the international scene was afforded by the research of the agricultural economist Theodore W. Schultz. As early as 1945, Schultz had developed a detailed critique of Western aid programs for industrializing nations which, he argued, were operating to the detriment of agriculture. He proposed that investment in elementary and secondary education and other reforms — rather than expenditures on imported machinery — could increase agricultural production, thereby staving off periodic cycles of rural starvation, as well as benefiting the nation as a whole. Under his leadership, detailed economic analysis was extended to such problems as fertility, marriage, crime, and human nutrition. Schultz's application of economic analysis to the agricultural plight of less-developed countries won him the Nobel Prize in economics in 1979.

The first faculty members to go to the Little University of Chicago in Frankfurt take off from the Chicago municipal (now Midway) airport as families and friends wave "bon voyage." From top to bottom in the back row are Wilhelm Pauck, Mrs. Louis Thurstone, Everett C. Hughes, and Roger B. Oake. In the front row are Paul A. Weiss, Louis Thurstone, Elder J. Olson, Margaret Ruth, and Mrs. Oake.

Turbulence in the 1960s

President Beadle (left) at a CORE *housing policy "sit-in" meeting, 1962*

A merican colleges in the eighteenth and nineteenth centuries were known for occasional student rebellions, usually over such homely issues as the quality of food and lodging or the strictness of parietal rules. Sometimes there were town-versus-gown riots. Founded late in the nineteenth century, the University escaped most of this uproar, and its emphasis on graduate study and research further limited the likelihood of serious academic unrest. The onset of the Depression and the approach of World War II, however, brought a new political urgency to academic discourse. In the 1930s and 1940s, University students staged strikes and demonstrations on such issues as peace and racial discrimination. In 1935 and again in 1951, the University successfully withstood investigation by legislators seeking subversive influences on the campus. The nonviolent nature of these events was typified by the single memorable student protest of the 1950s, which sprang from a curricular decision. Students assembled one evening outside the home of Chancellor Kimpton, in spirited but decorous objection to the reorganization of the four-year, general-education College.

After 1960, as national issues, especially civil rights and the Vietnam War, once again reached into campus life, decorum disappeared, along with the line that formerly separated the extracurricular from the academic. The "sit-in," the occupation of an academic building, became the conventional way to express opposition to a local or a national policy. At Chicago, for example, as early as 1962 members of the Student Government and the campus chapter of Congress of Racial Equality (CORE) occupied the anteroom of President Beadle's office to call attention to what they described as discriminatory practices in the University's rental of off-campus housing.

The next demonstration at Chicago arose from increased American involvement in Vietnam and the decision of the Selective Service System to use a student's academic standing in determining deferment or drafting. An organization called Students Against the

*On opposite page: Members of the University chapter of Congress of Racial Equality (*CORE*) stage a sit-in outside President Beadle's office, 1962*

Students protesting U.S. involvement in the Vietnam War march past the Administration Building, 1960s

Rank argued that providing this information to Selective Service involved an improper degree of complicity with national policy. On May 29, 1967, after a rally on the steps of the Administration Building, 120 students entered the building at 5:00 P.M. They vacated the building several hours later after being warned that those who remained might face stiff penalties, not excluding expulsion. Fifty-eight students were suspended for the Autumn Quarter for participating in the occupation; however, in most of the cases, the suspensions were not carried out, but instead were noted in the students' academic files.

The assassinations of Robert Kennedy and Martin Luther King, the subsequent urban riots, and the confrontation between antiwar demonstrators and Chicago police during the Democratic National Convention in August 1968 intensified feelings of crisis. The term "New Left" entered the national political vocabulary, and the Students for a Democratic Society (SDS) called for the restructuring of American society, starting with the academic "establishment." Ceremonial academic occasions became especially popular targets of political protest. Thus, on November 13, 1968, a civic dinner in downtown Chicago honoring the accession of Edward Hirsch Levi as the University's eighth President was the scene of protests by SDS and the Hyde Park Area Draft Resisters' Union. The demonstrators raised vociferous objection to the presence of the main speaker at the dinner, McGeorge Bundy, president of the Ford Foundation and former national security adviser to Presidents Kennedy and Johnson.

President Levi himself was deeply concerned about the future of the University in troubled times. "The growing acceptance of forms of protest, including violence, would in fact destroy the very idea of a university," Levi had stated in a speech to alumni earlier in the year. In answer to criticism from Saul Alinsky and other activists that the University was not "relevant" to contemporary political trends, Levi pointed to the role that disinterested scholarship plays in society. "A university is not a government," he explained:

Undue reliance upon universities as handy agencies to solve immediate problems, remote from education, can only end in corruption of the universities. And the danger is greater because corruption is easy and attractive, particularly when it is dressed up as a relevant response to the problems of our day. The danger is greater not because we should be against these activities, but on the contrary because we must be for many of them.

Two months after the inauguration of President Levi, the most stringent test of Chicago's internal governance came following a decision not to reappoint an assistant professor. The tenured faculty in the Department of Sociology had voted unanimously not to recommend the reappointment of Marlene Dixon for a second term, while the Committee on Human Development, where she was jointly appointed, had voted unanimously to recommend her reappointment, although there were differences of opinion as to the length of the second term. Reviewing the split decision, D. Gale Johnson, Dean of Social Sciences, recommended that Dixon not be reappointed. The Dean of Faculties, John T. Wilson, concurred.

A student leads the takeover of the Administration Building, 1969

On following pages: Students gather in front of the Administration building for "study-in," 1967

Critics promptly charged that Dixon was being released for one or more of the following reasons: that she was active in the New Left and had been a protester at the Levi inauguration, that she was a woman, or that faculty emphasis upon publication had overlooked her performance as a teacher. On January 23, 1969, the Dixon supporters issued an ultimatum:

We demand that (1) Marlene Dixon be rehired *jointly in Sociology and Human Development*, and (2) the principle of equal student control over hiring and rehiring of faculty, be accepted by the University no later than 9 A.M., Wednesday, January 29.

Unless these demands are accepted at this time, we will take militant action.

The threatened "militant action" followed at noon on January 30, when about four hundred persons seized the Administration Building. Within minutes, the staff evacuated the building and security guards were placed in the hallways. (Under the administration's instructions, the security guards were not armed and agreed not to "see or hear" any of the protesters.) Dean of Students Charles O'Connell issued a notice calling any occupation of the building a "disruptive" demonstration. Summonses were distributed to students who could be identified, asking them to appear within an hour before the Faculty Disciplinary Committee.

In this confrontation, as in others during the 1960s, the University's response depended upon the working of an internal governance system that had been in effect for a quarter of a century. Authorized by the Board of Trustees following controversy between faculty members and President Hutchins over the reorganization of the College, the system established a Senate consisting of virtually all members of the faculty, a fifty-one-member Council elected by the senators, and a seven-member Committee chosen by the Council. The Council of the Senate had regular monthly meetings; the Committee of the Council met more often. The President served as presiding officer of all three bodies. During emergencies such as that created by the sit-in, both the Council and the Committee were in session almost every day. University actions, including the institution and conduct of disciplinary procedures, were carried out under the aegis of these governing bodies. Thus, it proved difficult for the student protesters to focus upon the "administration" when demands were made upon the University. The faculty governance system provided a less attractive target. In addition, President Levi had called for the establishment of student-faculty consultative committees in all parts of the University down to the departmental level. These groups

THE MAROON

Volume 77, Number 31' 33   The Chicago Maroon   Friday, January 31, 1969

400 STUDENTS

OCCUPY AD BLDG!

David Travis

THE MAROON

Volume 77, Number 42   The Chicago Maroon   February 14, 1969

Sit-In Ends!

Students occupying the administration building have voted to end their two week old sit-in. A motion to leave the building within 24 hours passed by an overwhelming majority at a meeting in the building early Friday morning.

Earlier at that meeting, students had voted to modify the original demands of the sit-in. As of press time, it was not clear whether the group intended to maintain its demands after ending the sit-in.

They moved up to non-negotiable status three demands that were formerly stated "in principle." The demands are:

• End demolition, start construction in Woodlawn.

• Open a day care center for faculty children.

• Admit as students more Negroes, workers, and people from the "third world."

Students at the meeting favored a plan to assemble as many people as possible in the administration building and stage a dramatic mass exit Friday afternoon. There will be a rally in front of the building at noon. The students plan to leave the building at 4:30 pm.

Marlene Dixon, whose reappointment was the demonstrators' chief demand, made an appearance at the meeting, and talked briefly about the success of the sit-in.

The student power demand, which had been the most controversial inside and outside the two week sit-in, was dropped after little discussion. Only about a dozen voted to retain it.

DIXON WAS THE ONE: Marlene Dixon meets with a few of her supporters in the Register's office on Thursday.

O'Connell Issues 22 New Suspensions

A second report from the disciplinary committee to dean of students Charles O'Connell has resulted in the suspension of 22 more students charged with participating in the administration building sit-in.

A statement from O'Connell to students and faculty announced Thursday that these suspensions, like the 61 suspensions issued Feb 2, were sent to persons who "failed to discontinue a disruptive demonstration" and who failed to appear before the disciplinary committee after having been summoned."

In hearings since Feb 2, the disciplinary committee has lifted three of the 61 interim suspensions, bringing the total number of students suspended because of the 15-day sit-in to 80, O'Connell said.

One suspension was lifted upon evidence that a false ID card had been used. The other two cases involved situations in which students proved that they did not receive summonses in time to meet the stated deadline for making an appointment with the disciplinary committee.

Most of the suspended students have not yet contacted the disciplinary committee, which is regarded as an illegitimate body by many of the students in the sit-in. The disciplinary committee, chaired by law professor Dallin H. Oaks consists of nine faculty members and was appointed Jan 30 by the committee of the council of the faculty senate, the first day of the sit-in.

The committee also has four student observers.

The first 61 suspensions were issued to students who were handed summonses while actually in the administration building. Within the past week, however, the office of the dean of students has been issuing summonses to students identified as participating in the sit-in from photographs taken inside the administration building. Some of the 22 students suspended Wednesday may have been issued summonses in this fashion.

As with the original suspensions, the University administration will not publicly name the students being disciplined unless the individual requests a public hearing. The temporary suspensions will be in effect until the disciplinary committee resolves the case of the particular student involved.

Questioning at the special disciplinary committee hearing on Thursday afternoon concentrated on whether being in the administration building during a sit-in necessarily means being disruptive.

Jo Ann Winer, '71, said that she went into the administration building because "all my close friends were in the sit-in, and I wanted to talk to them at that time." "I was in there for personal reasons," she said "and I consider that any accusation that I was there for the purpose of being disruptive is invalid."

DEAN OF STUDENTS O'CONNELL: Looking forward to returning home to his cozy second floor administration building nook.

attended to local issues which could be settled through prompt student-faculty communication.

As February 1969 wore on, the original *casus belli,* the issue of Marlene Dixon's appointment, began to fade. On February 12, a faculty committee appointed to investigate the decision—a committee chaired by Hanna H. Gray, an Associate Professor of History—issued its report. The committee concluded that no violation of normal appointive procedures had occurred, and recommended that a one-year terminal reappointment be tendered to Dixon on the grounds that resolution of her status had been delayed by the controversy over her case. While Dixon did not accept this offer, neither did she publicly criticize the fairness of the Gray Committee.

On February 15, the occupants of the Administration Building voted to abandon their sit-in, although sporadic disturbances on and near the Quadrangles continued for the rest of the month. Meanwhile, the disciplinary committees continued their hearings. In mid-March they completed their final reports, providing this disposition of the cases before them: eighty-one persons suspended, forty-two expelled, three placed on probation, and one fined for the cost of a broken window. The disciplinary action was one of the most comprehensive among those at major universities affected by student disruptions in 1969. Trusting in its own system of governance, the University had refused to call in the police to maintain order; it also refused to grant ex post facto amnesty to violators of campus rules of conduct. The *New York Times* praised the University's handling of the crisis as the best in the nation. Others, including a group of parents of some of the expelled students, accused the University of "overkill."

Levi offered a temperate assessment of what had happened. In a written bulletin to faculty and students, he said, in part, that "the University has sought throughout this period, however imperfectly, to exemplify the values for which it stands. It has encouraged discussions through faculty and student groups. It has sought to institutionalize a process for wider participation." Then he added soberly:

In a world of considerable violence, and one in which violence begets violence, it has emphasized the persuasive power of ideas. It has sought—and the unique response of faculty and students has made this possible—to handle its own affairs in a way consistent with its ideals.

Edward H. Levi

The Humanities in the Twentieth Century

Humanists in the universities—people concerned with the study of literature, philosophy, history, classical and modern foreign languages, the arts—have always been willing to take the backward look, to examine the monuments of the human past with interest and affection. They have sought to guard and interpret the records of civilization. For them, a well-stocked library is the essential academic institution, and the abolition of memory is the ultimate cultural tyranny.

At Chicago, from the earliest years, solicitude for the preservation of the humanistic record was deeply ingrained. President Harper took the lead in assembling the classic Greek and Latin texts for the University Library. Scholars in medieval and Renaissance history have always been admired and influential members of the faculty, often in unusual ways. For instance, the foreign correspondent Vincent Sheean recalled how, during his College days, the Renaissance historian Ferdinand Schevill had stimulated his interest in Middle Eastern politics. In the study of modern literatures—English, Romance, Germanic—the prevalent philological emphasis placed heavy emphasis on early texts and their historical setting. In the Chicago Department of English, as at other universities, the dominant figures specialized in Anglo-Saxon, Chaucer, and Renaissance drama. The first Chicago Ph.D. dissertation on a topic in American literature was written in 1909.

Historical studies in the humanities have continued to flourish at Chicago. Literary history, musicology, and art history remained core disciplines, and drew new strength by the appointment of scholars attracted from European universities. However, during recent decades humanists at Chicago, like their colleagues elsewhere, explored imaginative ways of bridging the gap between past and present, of making humanistic creations more accessible to both students and adults. This was more than a mere matter of fleshing out reading lists with contem-

Richard P. McKeon

On opposite page: A humanities class listens to a slide lecture on classical sculpture, 1945

Saul Bellow

Carl Darling Buck

porary works and with books drawn from outside the familiar Western traditions. It involved the quest for useful perspectives to place alongside the established historical modes. The Great Books movement itself was one such venture. Two other important developments were the turn toward critical analysis in the study of literature and other arts, and a growing interest in the relationship between scholarship and creative performance.

Practitioners of the critical approach stressed close reading of texts and the inculcation of skills that would make this reading more penetrating. Advocates of what came to be called the "New Criticism" began to appear in humanities faculties from the late 1930s on. The Chicago variant of this movement was spearheaded by Richard P. McKeon, a philosopher and Dean of the Division of the Humanities, and Ronald S. Crane, a historian of eighteenth-century English literature before turning his attention to criticism. Among their students were Elder Olson, Bernard Weinberg, and Wayne C. Booth. Members of the group were sometimes known as neo-Aristotelians because of their admiration for the kind of interpretation practiced in Artistotle's *Poetics*.

In undergraduate instruction critical analysis quickly demonstrated its value in assisting students to understand humanistic works. The first-year Humanities course in the Chicago College generated three widely admired manuals of humanistic pedagogy titled *Learning to Look*, for the visual arts, *Learning to Listen*, and a handbook for literature that came to be known familiarly as *Learning to Litter*. Sometimes this emphasis on analytic skills led to certain grotesqueries: one faculty member was reported to have said (one hopes jocularly) that his aim was to teach Jane Austen's *Emma* so thoroughly that his students would never need to read another novel as long as they lived. By and large the Chicago critics coexisted productively with their colleagues of other persuasions: they prided themselves on being less hermetic in their interests than the New Critics.

The opening up of the curriculum brought about by the move toward criticism was accompanied by efforts to bring artistic creativity and performance more fully into the academic program. Here the Department of Music took the lead. While maintaining great distinction in musicology and music theory, Music enlarged its faculty in composition, and organized performing groups for a range of tastes from the Collegium Musicum to the Contemporary Chamber Players.

The physical transformation of the campus described in an earlier chapter also had its effect. The creation of the Goodspeed

Wayne C. Booth

Chamber Concert Orchestra, 1944

Elder Olson

recital hall, the opening of the Cochrane-Woods Art Center, and the housing of Court Theatre in its new, permanent quarters all enlivened the humanistic scene. Other resources were provided by activities in the Midway Studios and the Renaissance Society's exhibitions at Bergman Gallery in Cobb Hall. Even a relatively new art form, cinema, made its way into the curriculum. For many years a student group, Documentary Films, the oldest college film society in the country, maintained the cinematic presence on the Quadrangles with innovative screenings. With the appointment to the faculty of Gerald Mast, a film historian and critic, a cinema center was set up in Cobb Hall, and shortly thereafter the construction in 1986 of the Max Palevsky Cinema in Ida Noyes Hall gave the motion picture a proper showplace.

While these other modes of creativity moved into place, professors continued writing stories and poems just as they had been doing since the times of Robert Herrick and William Vaughn Moody. Saul Bellow and Richard Stern won acclaim with their novels and stories, and the latter directed a creative writing program. Elder Olson and A. K. Ramanujan were among other faculty who maintained the literary tradition. And Norman Maclean, a Professor of Literature and the only three-time winner of the Quantrell Award for excellence in undergraduate teaching, found his voice as a storyteller late in life, and enchanted readers with *A River Runs Through It*, a collection of stories about his youth in Montana.

As if to demonstrate that no generalizations about humanistic activity are unassailable, it should be noted that, simultaneously with these developments in criticism and creativity, another distinguished group of scholars was moving toward what the Europeans call the "humane sciences." This was the Department of Linguistics, a discipline at one time manned almost single-handedly by the eminent Indo-European philologist Carl Darling Buck. As the University expanded its instruction in non-Western languages after 1960, there was an influx of area specialists and linguistic theorists into the Department, which soon numbered more than twenty. Linguistics had an especially fruitful relationship with the social sciences, especially the Department of Anthropology. By a happy symmetry, just as its forerunner, philology, had nourished the history of the arts, so linguistics has had a powerful effect on the course of recent criticism.

Norman Maclean

The Pritzker School of Medicine and the Division of the Biological Sciences

The notable accomplishments of medicine in this century paralleled the incorporation of medical education into the university research framework. The University of Chicago was at the forefront of the revolution that transformed the field of medicine into a profession based on rigorous academic training and advanced scientific knowledge. In the early decades of the University, association between Rush Medical College and the Ogden School of Science foreshadowed this development.

The medical school that opened in 1927 on the Midway, now known as the Pritzker School of Medicine, represented further advances. It was located within the University community and reflected Chicago's orientation toward combining basic research with patient care and clinical teaching. Equipped with its own teaching hospital and inpatient and outpatient clinics, the medical school took students out of the lecture hall and into the wards and laboratories to the end of "making researches into the nature, cause, and treatment of disease," in the words of Dr. Frank Billings.

The faculty were a special breed selected to do more than make their rounds at the hospital, teach an occasional course, and derive their income from outside practice. From the beginning, the medical school embraced the "full-time" principle. Chicago remains unusually thoroughgoing among the major medical institutions in requiring all clinical faculty to be fully salaried, full-time employees of the University. This contrasts with the still fairly common practice in which doctors and surgeons supplement their hospital work with a private practice. In fact, to avoid the possibility that private practice might become a faculty member's chief preoccupation, all fees collected for professional services are paid to the University.

Various institutional arrangements further integrated medicine into the University structure. When Chicago was reorganized into divisions, medicine was made part of the Division of the Biological Sciences. This brought the clinical branches of medicine

Dr. Lowell T. Coggeshall

On opposite page:
Dr. Leon O. Jacobson

under one administrative roof with such basic science departments as Anatomy, Physiology, and Zoology. The reorganization was not without problems in adjusting to competing interests of the basic biological sciences and the clinical fields, but on the whole the tensions proved energizing to both groups. Within the clinics themselves, another organizational innovation was the development of the subspecialty system. Under the guidance of Franklin C. McLean and Russell M. Wilder, the Department of Medicine was organized into functional units—for example, Radiology, Dermatology, Neurology, Cardiology, and Clinical Chemistry—that proved highly valuable in advancing research.

As medical research and related clinical practice grew more sophisticated after World War II, the costs of university-based medicine escalated. Outside support and "third-party" payments for fees and services became more and more essential. The federal share of support for medical research rose from 7 percent in 1940 to 54 percent by 1957, health care subsidized by employers became prevalent in the middle class, and, in 1966, Medicaid extended basic health care to the poor, followed by Medicare for the elderly.

Chicago's role in this period was that of creating the special facilities needed to carry out its chief interest in advancing knowledge through research and discovery. Ten major medical buildings were added to the original four between 1950 and 1960, which more than doubled the size of the complex. Completion of the Bernard Mitchell Hospital in the 1980s rounded out the extensive medical center that had emerged west of the main campus during the preceding quarter-century. In addition, these years marked the almost continuous rebuilding of existing space to incorporate medical equipment, improved patient units, and redesigned laboratories.

The intermeshing of private and public decision making was a constant feature of this surge of medical growth. This was illustrated when Dr. Lowell T. Coggeshall, Dean of the Biological Sciences and later Vice-President of the University, who initiated the early expansion program, decided it was time to pursue research on the medical uses of atomic radiation. The idea for the Argonne Cancer Research Hospital (now the Franklin McLean Memorial Research Institute) came to Dr. Leon O. Jacobson shortly after he had completed his association with the Manhattan Project. Jacobson's experience with the biomedical effects of atomic energy convinced him that a special research unit would be highly beneficial. Discussions about funding a cancer isotope hospital were carried out with the National Cancer Institute, the National Institutes of Health, and the U.S. Public Health

The Bernard Mitchell Hospital

Medical students, 1970s

Service. The program came under the Atomic Energy Commission following an appropriation by Congress of several million dollars for cancer research. Dr. Cornelius Vermeulen recalled the negotiations involved in the establishment of the hospital:

At first, the location of the new facility was uncertain. Should it be on the campus or at the Argonne National Laboratory in Du Page County? The Director of the Argonne Laboratory suggested that the hospital should be located on the University campus, although the word "Argonne" would remain in the name. The plan that emerged after a visit by a governmental advisory committee in February 1948 was for a new building attached to the University medical complex. Ownership of the facilities would remain with the A.E.C., which would also be responsible for the operation and annual budget. On June 28, the University received a letter from the A.E.C. approving the plan, and University authorities acted upon it the same day. The arrangements thus became operative within the time limit imposed by Congress under which the A.E.C. was required to obligate its funds by June 30, 1948.

The facility was fully operational in 1953 under the direction of Jacobson. The use of radioactive isotopes in the diagnosis and treatment of cancer accelerated rapidly, with Argonne researchers contributing many discoveries. Dr. Paul Harper and Katherine A. Lathrop, for example, devised solutions of radioiodine in plastic vials for the treatment of cancer of the pancreas and behind the eye. They also developed radiostrontium needles to destroy tissue in the brain as a means of controlling the spread of breast cancer and various symptoms of Parkinson's disease. Dr. Alexander Gottschalk and his associates made important advances in cancer-detecting instrumentation. The isotope hospital developed scanners for use with experimental animals, a wide-area scanning technique with a scintillation camera, and a color television display with a three-dimensional display unit.

Complementing the isotope hospital was the Ben May Institute. Ben May became a world center for the study and treatment of cancer through chemicals. Dr. Charles Huggins, Director of the Institute, believed that cancer could best be treated not by surgery or X-ray but by drugs. He found that male or female hormones could bring improvements to patients with advanced cancer in the prostate and also of the breast. Among his many accomplishments was the development of the albumin test. Discovery that the albumin of blood was often markedly abnormal when a patient had cancer, he and his associates developed a blood test that gave a quicker, earlier identification of the disease. In 1966, Huggins was awarded the Nobel Prize for medicine for his long-term research.

Similar advanced facilities were made available for treatment and research in other specialties. During the expansive 1960s and

1970s alone, new units erected included the Chronic Disease Hospital, the Wyler Children's Hospital, the Surgery Brain Research Pavilion, and, on the north side of 58th Street at the Science Quadrangle, the Cummings Life Science Center, providing laboratories for biochemistry, biophysics, and microbiology.

At the same time that medical faculty members were developing these innovative centers for scientific investigation and treatment, they mustered energy and concern to address serious social and economic problems arising from the changing nature of health care on the South Side of Chicago. The flight of private physicians from the inner city had caused a crisis. In Woodlawn, the community south of the campus, the number of doctors had decreased by one-third as the population grew under the influx of black migration. The infant mortality rate was fifty-four per one thousand births, more than twice the national average.

Another indicator of the crisis in urban medical care was the explosive growth of emergency room visits. As recently as 1953, a single room at Billings had served as the emergency room of the hospital. In 1964, 25,000 visits were made to the enlarged emergency room suite in the new Gilman Smith Hospital; by 1972, the number had ballooned to 100,000. A second emergency room for children was established at Wyler Hospital.

In the summer of 1967, the University opened what is now the Woodlawn Maternal and Child Health Center to improve local health care. Supported by a grant from the Children's Bureau of the U.S. Department of Health, Education, and Welfare, the facility provided services without fee for residents of the Woodlawn community. It was designed to treat acute and chronic conditions in children and to provide preventative medical care. The Woodlawn Health Center has continued to serve the Woodlawn neighborhood and the communities of South Shore and Greater Grand Crossing. Staffed by six physicians, the Center, located on East 61st Street, is operated in conjunction with the Departments of Pediatrics and Obstetrics and Gynecology.

Dr. Charles Huggins

Helen Harris Perlman, School of
Social Service Administration

The Professional Schools

Just as the School of Medicine based its professional curriculum and clinical practice upon fundamental inquiry in the Division of the Biological Sciences, so the other graduate professional faculties undertook to strengthen their programs by drawing upon related fields of scholarship. A common assumption of the Chicago schools was that professional activity in the contemporary world would require practitioners to respond intelligently to rapid and sometimes unpredictable change, and that this capability could best be fostered by an education emphasizing the central disciplines underlying the profession.

The intellectual stance of the professional schools may be viewed in miniature by the efforts of the Graduate School of Business, the largest of the schools, to craft an M.B.A. curriculum appropriate to a fast-moving modern business environment. The chief architects of this reform were W. Allen Wallis and James H. Lorie. Wallis was a statistician and Chairman of the Statistics Department when he accepted Chancellor Kimpton's invitation to head the school.

Under the curricular changes initiated after 1956, M.B.A. candidates were required to take courses in the social sciences, including economics, applied mathematics, psychology, and sociology, in addition to marketing, finance, industrial relations, production, and other business courses. The idea was to deepen the students' knowledge of business with the insights of social scientists, to equip them to deal rationally with the uncertainties of the future. As Dean Wallis wrote, "Academic institutions can provide at best only pale and distorted reflections of actual business. The business of schools of business is preparing for lifelong learning from experience."

To implement the program, the Graduate School of Business attracted leading scholars from around the country. Among those recruited were psychologist Gary A. Steiner, social scientist Joel Seidman, and economist George J. Stigler, who solidified the school's identification with the orientation of the Department of Economics.

W. Allen Wallis

Harry Bigelow

George J. Stigler

In many cases the appointments were made jointly with other academic units. As Lorie recalled some years later:

We wanted—and got—top people. For example, I asked Al Rees to name the outstanding man in America in labor economics, someone who was senior but not old, and he said that man was George Shultz.... We went through the same process to get [Sidney] Davidson, without doubt the number one man in accounting in the country.

Shultz came to the school in 1957, following nine years as a labor economist at M.I.T. and with time as a labor arbitrator and senior economist for President Eisenhower's Council of Economic Advisers. Shultz pursued his research at Chicago, publishing *Public Policy and the Structure of Collective Bargaining*, and served as a consultant to President Kennedy's Advisory Committee on Labor Management Policy before being named Dean in 1962, succeeding Wallis, who became president of the University of Rochester. Shultz remained Dean until January 1969 when he left for Washington to become President Nixon's Secretary of Labor.

The school underwent tremendous growth during the Wallis, Lorie, and Shultz periods. In the ten years between 1955 and 1965, the budget increased fivefold, the faculty increased from thirty to seventy-nine, and enrollment in the Ph.D. and M.B.A. programs more than doubled. Finding enough space for students and faculty was difficult until Rosenwald Hall was remodeled and made the school's headquarters in 1972. It was during the 1960s that the school established its reputation as an international center for quantitative research. The Center for Mathematical Studies, jointly established by the Graduate School of Business and the Department of Economics, conducted a wide range of empirical studies into the behavior of the public and private sectors. The Center for Health Administration Studies became a leading group in examining the management, economics, and sociology of health services. Another center did significant work on the analysis of market investments. From this research came the provocative "random walks" theory that challenged the tradition of using pattern analysis to predict the stock market—a theory that challenged, troubled, and outraged stock analysts on Wall Street.

The Law School followed a similarly enterprising course. Building on the "New Plan" of Harry Bigelow and Wilber Katz, Dean Edward Levi fashioned a curriculum that developed significant connections between law and other disciplines, especially economics. A celebrated workshop on this interconnection, with Aaron Director as its mentor, explored the economic implications of such legal ques-

James H. Lorie

Following page: Law students during a tax law lecture, 1966

Harry Kalven

Soia Mentschikoff

tions as antitrust regulations, property and commercial law, and tax-ation policies.

Under Levi and his successors, the Law School expanded its work in both traditional and unconventional lines of inquiry. Before his recruitment into the Kennedy administration, Nicholas Katzenbach gave the school unique stature in space law. Walter Blum and Harry Kalven joined forces to write an outstanding legal essay, "The Uneasy Case for Progressive Taxation." Brainerd Currie taught in the field of conflict of law. Karl Llewellyn and Soia Mentschikoff joined Roscoe Steffen in the commercial law group. Hans Zeisel, a sociologist, led discussions on law and behavioral science.

Another expansion in the Law School's program took place in 1965 with the establishment of the Center for Studies in Criminal Justice. Aided by a major grant from the Ford Foundation, the center applied its legal expertise in the areas of corrections, the etiology of crime, aftercare, and the criminal justice system, developing strong links with policymakers around the country. Members of the center were involved in the Illinois Jails Survey and helped draft a new code of corrections for the State of Illinois. In 1971, the center established, with the University Press, a series of book-length publications devoted to significant contributions in criminology and criminal justice.

While the Law School's research projects explored the diverse ways in which law and the legal system acted upon social institutions, faculty members continued to give scrupulous attention to central questions of legal interpretation. Issues of constitutional law, especially those concerned with boundary lines between areas of judicial decision and political policy, were frequently weighed in essays by professors, students, and graduates of the school. Some of these essays sounded themes counseling judicial restraint that would be taken up later by Judge Robert Bork, J.D. '53, and Associate Supreme Court Justice Antonin Scalia, both of whom had taught at the school.

As an earlier section of this narrative made clear, from its beginnings the School of Social Service Administration was commit-ted both to working for the amelioration of social conditions and to using scholarly inquiry as its principal instrument in this mission. As one observer noted of Edith Abbott and Sophonisba Breckinridge, the founders of the school, "Their commitment to reform [was] no less intense than that of other prominent leaders in the settlement-house movement, but they were first and foremost scholars and teach-ers. The classroom and the pen became the tools of activism."

The faculty of Social Service Administration responded to criticism of social work in the 1960s by trying to devise more effective strategies for dealing with current problems. The massive Midway Project examined the delivery system of the Cook County Department of Public Aid. The Center for the Study of Welfare was designated by the Department of Health, Education, and Welfare as a regional research institution, and a H.E.W. grant allowed the center to bring fellows from many academic disciplines to develop new types of social welfare research investigation. And with plain candor, *Social Service Review,* the journal edited by S.S.A. faculty, detailed the self-questioning that was stirring the social work profession.

In working out a productive relationship between professional education and scholarly inquiry, the situation of the Divinity School was particularly complex and challenging. From colonial times in America, the roles of the pastor and the schoolmaster had been closely intertwined, and for two centuries the shaping of the college curriculum had been influenced by the desire to ensure the presence of a scholar in the pulpit. Two of the first three Presidents of the University of Chicago had been biblical scholars, learned in philology as well as in scriptural exegesis. Many members of the Divinity School faculty worked closely over the years with humanists and social scientists, and sometimes held joint appointments in other divisions.

Because of this emphasis on scholarship, the Divinity School always attracted large numbers of students interested in preparing for careers in education rather than in the ministry. Those wishing to become professors of religion at the college level elected Ph.D. programs in church history, history of religion, or theology. Others, by combining Divinity School requirements with advanced courses and research in cognate fields, became college professors of sociology, or psychology, or literature. By 1960, most of the Divinity School's students were enrolled in Ph.D. programs rather than in the traditional bachelor of divinity curriculum.

However, the school was not prepared to relinquish its role in professional education. In 1966, a new doctor of ministry degree was authorized as the capstone of an entirely new professional curriculum. Nearly two decades of experience with this revised program led, in 1983, to the institution of a three-year master of divinity as the basic degree for students planning to enter the ministry. The doctor of ministry degree remained as an advanced degree for ministry students who wished to extend their education under the school's nondenominational and interdisciplinary approach. At the same time, a new Ph.D. program in Practical Theology was approved. According to the faculty mandate, Practical Theology "would investigate critically religious claims, on the one hand, and social scientific inquiries, on

Edward Levi at microphone, ca. 1970

the other, with respect to their import for particular problems of [religious] practice."

The concerns prompting these curricular experiments were a reflection, at least in part, of changing patterns of recruitment for the ministerial profession. These patterns were influenced, in turn, by the growth of religious fundamentalism during recent decades. The development of fundamentalism within the world's religions led to a major research effort at Swift Hall under the direction of Martin Marty. Established through a grant by the John D. and Catherine T. MacArthur Foundation, the study involved scholars from around the world who presented research on Protestant, Islamic, Roman Catholic, and Sikh fundamentalism, as well as similar movements in Judaism, Buddhism, and other religions. The first of several international conferences was held at the University in November 1988, with scholars attempting to define characteristics common among the various forms of fundamentalism. Five volumes of research reports, under the general title "Fundamentalism Observed," are expected from the project.

In all the professional fields reviewed here, the University's view of its educational function has been affected by changes within the professions themselves. In two areas of professional education, the late 1980s witnessed especially striking modifications in this view. For many years the Graduate Library School had pioneered in investigating innovative techniques of librarianship. In the Chicago pattern the Library School's work had drawn inventively upon scholarship in the

social sciences and humanities generally, and in computer science and linguistics particularly. Modes of improving cataloging, information retrieval, and the organization of knowledge were prime topics of inquiry for the school. However, with growing sophistication in the use of the computer, these matters were no longer uniquely concerns of library science; they had become part and parcel of graduate education generally. Under the changed circumstances the Library School found it difficult to attract students of the quality its program demanded, and the University reluctantly decided to withdraw from the professional education of librarians.

At the same time, the University was moving cautiously toward the establishment of a new professional school providing an interdisciplinary education for men and women who would be called upon to deal with questions of public policy. Issues of this kind had been taken up piecemeal in many departments and professional schools — Political Science, Law, Business, Social Service Administration. Half a century earlier, political scientists Charles Merriam and Leonard White had encouraged research on topics of current concern. The Center for Public Administration at 1313 East 60th Street had long been a presence on the edge of the Quadrangles. But it was now becoming apparent that the complexities of modern government required the best talents of people unfazed by problems not susceptible to conventional analysis and treatment. So, after several years of experimentation with an active Committee on Public Policy Studies, the University approved the transformation of this unit into the full-fledged Irving B. Harris Graduate School of Public Policy Studies.

Dean of the Divinity School Joseph Kitagawa, left, and Anthony Yu

On opposite page: Martin Marty

Students studying in Regenstein Library

Graduate Education in a Time of Scarcity

Along with other human institutions, universities have struggled to discover the uses of adversity. They, too, found consolation in the reminder that if you are stuck with a lemon you should prepare to make lemonade. A senior administrator at Chicago in the 1950s was fond of fending off importunate deans by recalling how, during the Depression, he and a fellow graduate in microbiology, staggered by an estimate of several hundred dollars for research equipment, walked down 57th Street to Wehrwein's Hardware Store, made a few purchases, and put together the necessary apparatus for $14.57. Economic austerity during the years of the Depression and World War II created a climate of urgency and assessment of priorities which fostered the University's curricular reforms during this period. As a parallel, Columbia University's experiment in general education had been inspired by a course in U.S. war aims during World War I.

Another major shift in the economic underpinnings of higher education confronted the University in the late 1970s. After two decades of steady growth, graduate education nationally was sliding into a period of severe contraction. The maturation of the "baby boom" generation transformed the demographic basis of American higher education, depriving colleges of increasing enrollments at the very time that faculty members appointed in the boom years were still far from retirement.

As a premier institution of graduate education preparing young scholars for academic careers, Chicago witnessed the changing demographics with understandable trepidation. Applications and enrollments in three of the four divisions (Social Science, Physical Sciences, and Humanities) had fallen off sharply. Between the Depression and the early 1970s, divisional enrollments had accounted for 40 percent or more of the University's student population. After 1972, the proportion of graduate enrollments declined steadily, down to 34 percent in 1978–79 and 30 percent in 1980–91. And, of course, even more worrisome than these alarming statistics was the possibility that the decline in numbers portended an erosion in quality, as talented college graduates looked toward nonacademic careers.

The future of graduate education was perhaps the foremost challenge facing Hanna H. Gray when she was named tenth President of the University in 1978. "In a way," she recalled later, "almost the identity or self-definition of the University as it had existed over the years was to some degree threatened, or questioned, as part of the national phenomenon. The University would have to make important decisions about how to approach these issues of graduate education, whether to devote fewer resources to it, whether to contract deliberately."

President Hanna H. Gray

President Gray appointed a faculty commission to examine local and national trends in graduate education, with a mandate to evaluate alternatives for future graduate work, including the possible restructuring of Ph.D. programs for students pursuing nonacademic careers. The commission, headed by Keith M. Baker, a historian, produced a comprehensive study in 1982, providing a precise assessment of the problems facing the nation's universities, a rationale for the improvement of the Chicago program, and a number of detailed recommendations for reform.

The Baker Commission report accepted the prediction that Ph.D. programs were likely to remain underenrolled nationwide in the conceivable future. It also anticipated a continued decline in financial support for higher education by government and foundations. The commission warned that Ph.D. graduates would face intense competition for available academic jobs in the future, and that a substantial segment of this group would move into nonacademic careers.

This sober appraisal laid before its readers, the Baker report firmly rejected the expedients of scaling back the University's commitment to graduate education or of adjusting the program toward narrowly focused utilitarian training. Rather, the report challenged the faculty and administration to marshal their resources to continue to attract the best students, to educate them well, and to assert the enduring importance of scholarship.

Graduate education will succeed to the extent that it enables its recipients not simply to solve given problems but to identify and create new questions; it will fail to the extent that it is merely training in a narrow specialization. Thus, it is our claim for graduate education, properly conceived, that it constitutes a true education, not simply an advanced form of professional training. This kind of education is best accomplished in an environment that combines a broad intellectual discipline with an emphasis upon research as the principal activity.

Under President Gray's leadership, the Baker Commission report did not remain simply a document on file. Its major recommendations for reform in the graduate program were promptly taken up by the appropriate academic bodies and put into effect within a year. Ph.D. candidates were encouraged to enter upon full-fledged doctoral research "as quickly, as clearly, and as self-consciously as possible." Therefore, the University dropped the traditional requirement of twenty-seven courses (three years of course work) before undertaking doctoral research. Financial aid programs were revamped to give more students an opportunity to maintain, without interruption, their schedule of study and research. The package of reforms tackled in a particularly innovative manner a problem identified by the Baker Commission in its investigations: following the completion of course work and formal admission to Ph.D. candidacy, many students were left largely on their own, "with no real opportunity or impulse to expose their ideas or written material to critical discussion." To remedy this deficiency, the University authorized the establishment of regular faculty-student workshops, on both departmental and interdepartmental bases, for discussions of ongoing doctoral work. By 1988, the number of students enrolled in the workshops had reached more than six hundred. Nearly one hundred faculty members were engaged in the program.

Spurred in part by the reforms, Chicago's four divisions began registering steady gains in applications and enrollments. From a low of two thousand in the 1982–83 period, the number of graduate students increased to 2,800 in 1988, "which is about as large as we probably ought to be," according to President Gray. The demographic horizon was also changing, opening up job opportunities for graduate students as faculty members appointed in the 1960s neared retirement. Chicago was well situated, Gray noted, to offer the kind of education required in these new circumstances:

The issue is not going to be in the next decade the dearth of opportunity for young scholars and teachers. The issue is going to be whether we have enough young scholars and teachers, especially of the kind of quality who should become the leaders of the next academic generation.

Chicago's ready and comprehensive response to the crisis in graduate education was quite in keeping with its characteristic mode of maintaining academic identity during times of stress and challenge. As a moderately sized private university with an abiding dedication to the trivium of scholarly inquiry, exemplary graduate education, and superior undergraduate liberal education, Chicago has had to ponder

Jane Overton teaching a class on cell structure development, 1970s

its priorities. Painstaking study, as was the case with the Baker Commission, has preceded resolute action.

Sometimes this awareness of priorities led the University not to do certain things, to refrain from entering fields of study worked energetically by many other universities, for example, professional studies in engineering, journalism, and the performing arts. Particularly wrenching were decisions to withdraw from activities in which the University had been an impressive pioneer but which were now carried on more effectively elsewhere: correspondence courses, home economics, nursing education, library science, geography, even big-time football. However, when fresh lines of inquiry attracted lively minds, the University was quick to react to these needs with new departments, institutes, and research groups in areas ranging from computer science and statistics to non-Western civilizations and public policy. As Thorstein Veblen had noted sardonically at the beginning of the century, the good gray Gothic of the first buildings was a standing rebuke to simple infatuation with novelty, but throughout its years the University has shown a willingness to be convinced that the new might also be the consequential.

On opposite page: Graduate Workshop in the History of Human Science, in the John Hope Franklin Room (the History Commons) in the Social Sciences Building, 1984

The Climate of Inquiry

Inevitably, much of the foregoing narrative, following as it does a paper trail through the archives of the University, becomes an account of men and women acting in groups. Academic organizations—divisions, departments, committees—are proficient in producing reports, minutes, evaluative summaries. This documentation is aliment for the archives.

As a grace note to this story, something should be added. Most students have had the experience of reaching an impasse in their research, then browsing aimlessly along the shelves of a great library, and hitting upon just the right volume by what seems pure chance. The happy stroke that scholars call serendipity befalls the prepared mind in a favoring environment. Chicago has been a hospitable place for highly individual curiosity, as well as a center of big science and the unending quest for multimillion-dollar research grants.

The University's habit of seeking out exploratory minds was emphasized by economist Milton Friedman in remarks made in 1974 to the Board of Trustees:

As we face financial pressure in the coming years, it is well to recall that the schools that developed at Chicago owed far more to a handful of geniuses than to the lavish expenditure of funds. The availability of funds certainly helped. But far more crucial was the success of the faculty in seeking out the young scholars who had within them the capacity to strike out in new directions and the willingness of the administration to back the faculty's judgment.

Often these exemplary individuals did their work within an institutional setting, but they did so with such flair that they changed the environment around them. Thus, several generations of strong-minded editors left their mark upon the Oriental Institute's Assyrian Dictionary as that compendium of ancient Mesopotamian civilization moved majestically through the decades. As relief from his labors on the dictionary, editor Leo Oppenheim wrote the study, *Ancient Mesopotamia*, which won the first Gordon Laing prize offered by the University of Chicago Press for the best book of the year by a Chicago

Sewall Wright

On opposite page:
The Humanities Quadrangle

Sir William Craigie

Henry C. Cowles's class on a field trip, 1911

faculty member. Sewall Wright, a zoologist, was another winner of the Laing prize for a volume published when he was in his ninth decade and had been long retired from the faculty. Wright approached fundamental problems in evolutionary biology with such originality and depth that his research papers continued to command scientific interest throughout his long lifetime.

Statesmen and generals have mountains named after them, but an early twentieth-century Chicago botanist has had his work memorialized in the designation of a bog forty miles east of the University. This is Cowles Bog, an area of prime scientific importance in the Indiana Dunes National Lakeshore. A pioneer of ecological science, Henry C. Cowles used the Indiana dunes and adjacent wetlands as his laboratory. His studies of the ecological significance and fragility of this stretch of Lake Michigan's southern coastline played a major role in the decision to establish the National Lakeshore. Biology students in the College continue to visit Cowles Bog on field trips.

Sometimes even research projects of limited duration brought to the Quadrangles unusual scholars who remained to enliven the scene after the original occasion for their presence had passed. In the 1930s, the University, perhaps seeking lexicographical balance with the Assyrian Dictionary already projected, decided to proceed with the preparation of a dictionary of American English. Sir William Craigie, fresh from work with the *Oxford English Dictionary,* was summoned to Chicago to try his hand with the American vocabulary. The job was done, the dictionary was published by the University Press, and Sir William returned to Great Britain. Fortunately, when the dictionary team was dispersed, there stayed behind one of Craigie's assistants, a courtly southerner named Mitford M. Mathews, who seemed to know everything there was to know about American turns of speech. Mathews's formal position was that of a Press editor in charge of bringing out additional scholarly volumes, such as his notable *Dictionary of Americanisms.* However, his real role emerged as a guide for perplexed students and faculty members buffaloed by the quirks of American usage. Cordially and lucidly, he reviewed for his questioners the possible meanings and etymologies of "copacetic" and "bodacious" and even more bizarre Americanisms. He was an authentic resource person.

Fascination with the American vernacular also inspired the scholarly career of one of Mathews's contemporaries, the literary scholar Walter Blair. Long before it became fashionable to study seriously the artifacts of popular culture, Blair was investigating nineteenth-century American humor, frontier folklore, and the fabri-

Subrahmanyan Chandrasekhar

*Mitford M. Mathews with his dictionary
on the Quiz Kids program*

George Beadle

cation of tall tales. He deepened the interpretation of the American literary record by showing how this vernacular vein underlay the achievement of many subsequent writers from Mark Twain to William Faulkner. Blair's active career spanned most of this century. In his eighty-fifth year, the University of California Press published the definitive edition of *The Adventures of Huckleberry Finn*, of which he was coeditor. In his ninetieth year he was pleased to learn that California schoolchildren were excitedly reading his *Tall Tale America*, published half a century earlier.

Vivacious curiosity and a broad spectrum of intellectual sympathies were characteristics common to these scholars of pronounced individuality. This was certainly the case with Subrahmanyan Chandrasekhar, whose researches in astrophysics earned him the Nobel Prize. Chandrasekhar took the occasion of delivering the 1975 Ryerson Lecture to identify the three great figures whose achievements seemed most impressive to him. Not surprisingly, one of the three was Newton. The other two were Beethoven and Shakespeare. Just as Keats, looking for a simile to express his response to a first reading of a translation of Homer, likened himself to "some watcher of the skies when a new planet swims into his ken," so the Chicago astronomer, seeking to convey his understanding of supreme human powers, found it in the linked trio of the physicist, the composer, and the dramatist.

A telling example of the persistent inquisitiveness that fuels inquiry accompanied George Beadle to Chicago when he became the seventh President of the University. A Nobel Prize–winning geneticist, Beadle brought with him a piece of unfinished business: what were the genetic stages by which primitive varieties of Mexican maize moved toward the corn plant of the present day? To this question he addressed himself whenever he could sequester a few hours free of the demands of the presidency. He located a small plot of vacant land at the edge of the campus and cultivated there some of the plants that he thought might be ancestors of modern corn. He carried out hybridization, and even persuaded some of his faculty colleagues to join in the experiment by chewing away at cornbread baked from the resulting crop. One man's scrap of earth near Ellis Avenue became a reminder of the oneness in spirit that the University undertook to cherish.